Project Finance

IFR
BOOKS

Project Finance

Clifford Chance

IFR Publishing Ltd

IFR Publishing, 11 New Fetter Lane, London EC4A 1JN

Reprinted 1994

British Library Cataloguing in Publication data available

ISBN 1 873446 45 4

Printed by Total Graphics Ltd, Edmonton, London N18

Contents

List of figures and tables

Checklists

Foreword

Project finance is a specialist area of international finance that, perhaps more than most, demands of its practitioners a flexible and imaginative approach to problem solving and, frequently, a capacity for lateral thinking.

Many projects require massive amounts of funding and involve high risks. The range of parties involved can include governments, development agencies, export credit bodies, suppliers, purchasers and contractors as well as borrowers and lenders. Their interests in making the venture a success might derive from quite different sets of priorities. Their willingness — and capacity — to accept risk will depend not just upon the financial interest that they have vested in the project but also upon the legal, political and economic environment in which they are operating. Basic assumptions about, for example, taking security or enforcing obligations may need to be revised to take account of local laws and legal systems.

It has been said that there are as many types of project finance as there are projects. Chapter 1 sets out to identify the characteristic features of a project financing and considers some of the misunderstandings that might arise from adopting too rigid or too simplistic an approach.

Chapters 2, 3 and 4 consider the range of structures that might be employed in project finance and the risks that must be addressed by all the parties concerned.

Chapters 5 and 6 focus more directly on the concerns of lenders: what are their requirements in terms of legal documentation and in terms of taking security? What other forms of support are available to cover the risks of project failure or unexpected political or economic change?

Chapter 7 examines some selected problem areas to illustrate the difficulties that might be encountered in striking a balance of risks and responsibilities that is acceptable to all parties.

The concluding chapter — Chapter 8 — looks to the future: to some of the potential "growth areas" for project finance, including Central and Eastern Europe, China and South East Asia.

For ease of reference, a glossary of some of the technical terms used in connection with project finance is set out in the Appendix.

This book is not a legal textbook. It does not purport to provide legal advice nor a comprehensive review of the legal framework in those regions where projects are being carried out. What it endeavours to do is to highlight some of the distinctive features of project finance — its concern with risk allocation, its adaptability to new and unfamiliar circumstances and, above all, its apparently infinite variety.

The position is stated as at June 1991.

Clifford Chance, July 1991

Chapter 1: Introduction

(1) What is project finance?

The term "project finance" is used to refer to a wide range of financing structures which have one feature in common: the financing is not primarily dependent on the credit support of the sponsors or the value of the physical assets involved. In a project financing, those providing the senior debt place a substantial degree of reliance on the performance of the project itself. As a result, they will concern themselves closely with the feasibility of the project and its sensitivity to the impact of potentially adverse factors.

A successful structure will entail a satisfactory and economic allocation of project risk among the various interested parties. In addition to the project sponsors and the senior lenders, risk might be accepted to a greater or lesser extent by suppliers of raw materials or equipment, contractors, operators, product purchasers or end users, insurers and government agencies (including export credit agencies). The extent to which any party will be willing to accept project risk depends on the return it anticipates it will receive. As an extension of this, the price required by different parties for taking a specific risk can vary significantly. Some risks might be unacceptable to some parties regardless of the potential rewards.

In the case of banks, it is certainly true that they will rarely enter into a project financing without some form of commitment on the part of the project sponsors. In some cases this might simply take the form of an equity investment in the project company. In others it might involve arrangements that, whilst not amounting to outright on-balance-sheet guarantees, represent tangible credit support collateral to, but not dependent on, the performance of the project.

Whilst there is no strict definition of "project finance", the term implies a financing that involves:

- some element of reliance on project assets and cash flows without full recourse to the sponsors or, in some cases, the borrower;
- specialist technical and economic evaluations of the project, the project sponsors' or operators' business and thorough on-going monitoring by the lender;
- complex loan and security documentation, quite probably involving innovative structures; and

- higher margins and fees to reflect the lender's exposure to project — and often political — risk.

(2) How does project finance differ from other kinds of limited recourse asset-based finance?

Comparisons can be made between project financing and limited recourse asset-based financing, particularly in the context of the security structures employed.

For example, loans to acquire and/or redevelop property are sometimes structured so that the lender has no right of recourse to the borrower except to the extent of the proceeds of sale of the specific property and the income derived from it. Such a loan would be secured by a mortgage over the property and an assignment of rents payable under the leases.

Ships are often financed on the basis of long-term transportation agreements or bareboat charterparties where a mortgage and an assignment of earnings and insurances form the only security.

Likewise, in project finance it is usual for the security to take the form of a mortgage of the project's physical assets and an assignment of the rights to the cash flow from the project.

Project finance, however, requires the consideration of other factors, relating to the technical feasibility of the project (the technical test) and its economic viability (the economic test). In the case of the technical test, the technology involved might be more sophisticated than, for example, that involved in a ship or property construction and the completion risk is thus much greater. In the case of the economic test, the value of the physical assets comprising the project might be substantially lower than the monies advanced and therefore the project's economic viability will be crucial.

In addition, there is a need to decide how the risks associated with the project are to be allocated between the lenders and the other parties. These risks might be divided differently as the project progresses from one stage to the next.

(3) The technical test

In satisfying itself as to the technical feasibility of a project, a bank will usually rely on a feasibility study put together by independent experts such as mining engineers, oil engineers or construction consultants. There is a preference for the adoption of tried and tested technology.

The role of the experts is crucial: for example, in the case of a project to construct a road, bridge or tunnel, the expert will scrutinise design and construction schedules, review traffic flow forecasts and the feeder infrastructure. In the case of a power station, the focus will be on the design and operating proposals; there will be a review of start-up test procedures, completion criteria and the availability of the necessary transmission infrastructure and grid capacity, as well as an assessment of fuel supply, consumption proposals and grid requirements. Most major banks have in-house technical experts who are often engineers with a career background in industry. Whilst the in-house experts can play an important role in protecting the lenders' interests, most lenders will still want to see an independent engineer involved in the assessment and monitoring of the project.

(4) The economic test

The economic test must show that, on the basis of cash flow projections, sufficient cash will be generated by the project to pay for all operating expenses, debt service, taxes, royalties and other costs (with an ample cushion for contingencies such as changes in exchange and interest rates, inflation and market demand) and to leave a surplus for the project company to meet its target for return on equity.

(5) What kinds of projects are "project-financed"?

The techniques of project finance are applied to a wide range of ventures, from the development of oil and gas fields and other natural resources to the construction and operation of luxury hotels and major agricultural developments.

Large-scale infrastructure projects — power generating stations, roads, railways and airports — account for much of today's project finance activity, particularly in the newly industrialised countries of South East Asia. In these projects, the "build-operate-transfer" (BOT) structure is often used and an assessment of the political as well as the purely economic risk over the long term is particularly important.

(6) What are the reasons for choosing project finance?

Project finance is more expensive than conventional financing because of:

- the time spent by the lenders, their technical experts and their lawyers in evaluating the project and negotiating the (usually very complex) documentation;
- the increased insurance cover, particularly consequential loss and political risk cover, which might be required;
- the costs of monitoring technical progress and performance and policing the loan during the life of the project; and
- the charges made by the lenders (and, possibly, other parties) for assuming additional risks.

The advantages to the project sponsors and operators must therefore be substantial to compensate for these additional costs. The more common reasons for borrowers opting for project finance are risk sharing, political risks, accounting treatment, restrictions on borrowing and tax benefits.

(a) Risk sharing

Where debt is wholly or partially non-recourse to the borrower and sponsors, all or some of the risks will be borne by the lenders if the project fails to produce sufficient cash flow. This is an important factor where the borrower is small in relation to the size of the project. Project failure will not necessarily bankrupt the borrower or the project sponsors.

(b) Political risks

A business investing large sums overseas might wish to ensure that certain political risks — such as price regulation, taxation, import and/or export barriers, preferment of competitors, expropriation or nationalisation — are borne by the lenders in respect of the loan finance.

(c) Accounting treatment

More conventional forms of borrowing might have a greater adverse effect on the borrower's — or the project sponsor's — balance sheet than the techniques used in project financing. This is particularly true where the financing is non-recourse.

Commitments of sponsors under take-or-pay, tolling or throughput agreements or other arrangements, even where they correspond in commercial terms to guarantees, do not always appear as such in the balance sheet or the notes to the accounts.

(d) Restrictions on borrowing

Where a sponsor has borrowing restrictions in its articles of association or in its existing credit facility documentation, it might be necessary or desirable to employ a finance structure that is not legally classified as a "borrowing", such as a forward purchase agreement, trustee borrowing or production payment arrangement.

(e) Tax benefits

The existence of tax allowances for capital expenditure and tax holidays for new enterprises might encourage project sponsors to think in terms of project finance. To take advantage of the tax holiday it might be necessary to set up a project company in the jurisdiction where the project will be physically located. Often, this company will be the borrower and all the project assets will be isolated within this borrowing vehicle. The structure of the financing might be driven by tax considerations, as shown by the development in the US of production payment techniques (described in more detail in Chapter 3(4)). The availability of capital allowances on plant and machinery in the UK has encouraged the use of finance leases within a project finance structure, as outlined in Chapter 3(6).

(7) Common misconceptions about project finance

The assumption that lenders should in all circumstances look to the project as the exclusive source of debt service and repayment is one misconception about the nature of project finance that can make negotiations between project sponsors, governments and lenders problematic. Other examples of over-simplification or misunderstanding include:

- *Lenders do not require a high level of equity investment from the project sponsors.* In fact, lenders frequently do look for substantial capital injections by the sponsors — to ensure a high degree of commitment to the project and to ensure that the sponsors are subordinated to the lenders and to reduce the project's overall level of debt service obligations. Project finance is not the same thing as venture capital. Subordinated loans will often be acceptable in place of equity and there might be advantages to sponsors in making their funds available in this way.

- *Project loans are 100% secured on the assets of the project.* Whilst lenders normally do take "belt and braces" security on project assets as well as cash flows, the realisable value of such assets alone might be negligible in the case, for example, of roads, tunnels and pipelines which cannot be moved or which cannot be used for any purpose other than in connection with the particular project. The value of a non-operating power station or petrochemical complex is likely to be far less than the cost of building it. Security is often taken primarily for "defensive" reasons — to prevent third parties interfering with the project — rather than with the intention of providing a realistic method of ensuring repayment. Equally, the objective of taking security might be to permit a sale of the business as a going concern.

- *The technical and economic performance of the project will be measured objectively according to pre-set tests and targets.* Lenders will always seek to reserve for themselves an element of discretion as to the satisfaction of performance conditions, particularly where these "tests" shift the financing from a recourse to a non-recourse basis. Borrowers will argue for objective tests to ensure that the transformation occurs automatically, unhindered by subjective value judgments on the part of the lenders.

- *The risk of project failure is shared equally by the lenders and the project sponsors.* Lenders will not want to see the abandonment of a project so long as some surplus cash flow is being generated over operating costs, even if this level represents an uneconomic return to the project sponsors on the resources and manpower dedicated to the project.

- *Lenders assume political risks in project finance.* Lenders will often seek assurances from the host government about the risks of expropriation and availability of foreign exchange; often these risks are covered by insurance or export credit guarantee support, the costs of which are (usually) ultimately borne by the project and project sponsors. The involvement in a project of multilateral organisations such as the World Bank or regional development banks might alleviate a lender's concerns about political risk to some degree.

Chapter 2: Organisation of project finance

(1) The parties involved

(a) The project sponsors

The sponsors might be one company or a consortium of interested parties, such as contractors, suppliers, purchasers or users of the project's product or facilities. Sponsors could include parties with indirect interests, such as the owners of land through which new transport facilities are to be built and who expect the value of their property to increase.

(b) The project company

The identity, domicile and legal form of the entity that will operate the project will be determined by a range of factors. First and foremost, the legal framework of the host country might prescribe the structures for foreign investment: it might not be possible for foreign entities to do business at all; there might be requirements for local participation in the establishment of joint ventures or new companies in the host country. Concepts of limited liability, partnership and common ownership might be different from those with which the sponsors are familiar. This could influence the ownership structure and the relations between the sponsors, as set out in the joint venture agreement or shareholders' agreement.

Ownership structures might also be dictated by the tax regimes and foreign exchange rules of the host country and, equally, by those of the domiciles of the project sponsors.

(c) The borrower

The borrowing entity might or might not be the same as the project company. Again, the structure of the financing and of the operation of the project will be determined by a range of considerations including tax, exchange controls, the availability of security and the enforceability of claims in the host country. In one project, there could be several "borrowers", each raising funds separately to cover its individual participation in the venture; for example, the construction company, the operating company, suppliers of raw materials to the project or purchasers (off-takers) of the project's production.

The borrower might be a vehicle specially established for the purpose: for example, in recent Indonesian oil projects, the use of a "trustee borrowing vehicle" (TBV) has been developed, in view of the restrictions on state entities' powers to borrow or to give guarantees. The TBV is established as a trustee for the state-owned entity, in this example a petroleum company. A simplified version of the TBV structure is outlined in Figure 1.

Figure 1: The TBV structure

(a) Construction

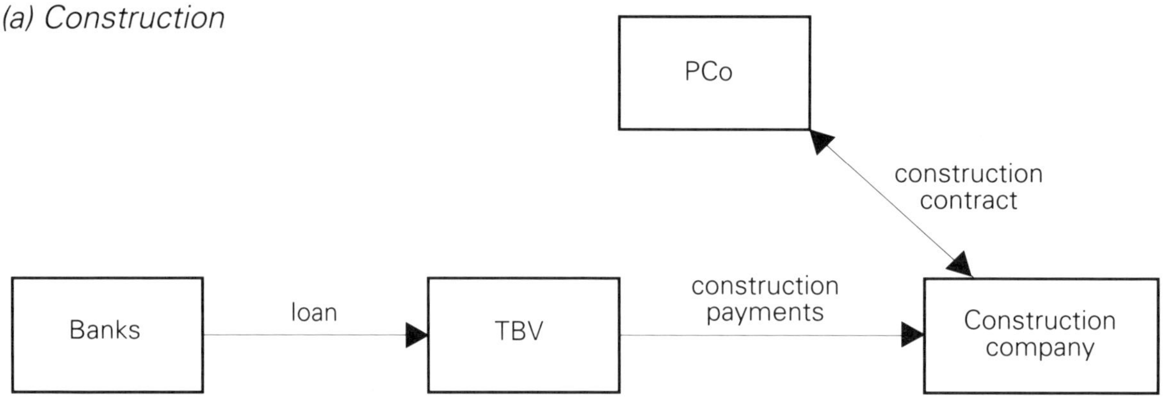

1. Banks finance the construction costs of the state-owned petroleum company (PCo) by making a loan to the TBV, which disburses funds to the construction company.

(b) Off-take

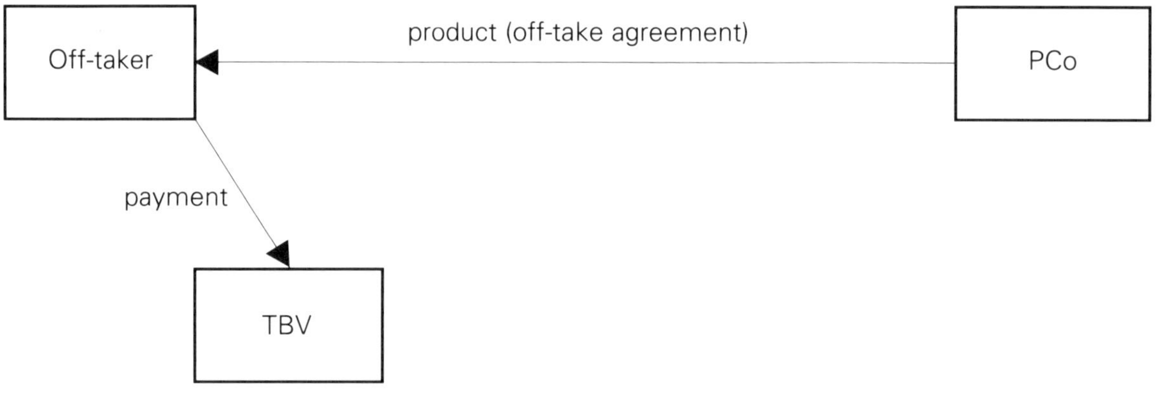

2. PCo has an off-take agreement with "off-taker" on a take-or-pay basis; PCo instructs off-taker to make all payments to TBV.

(c) Debt service

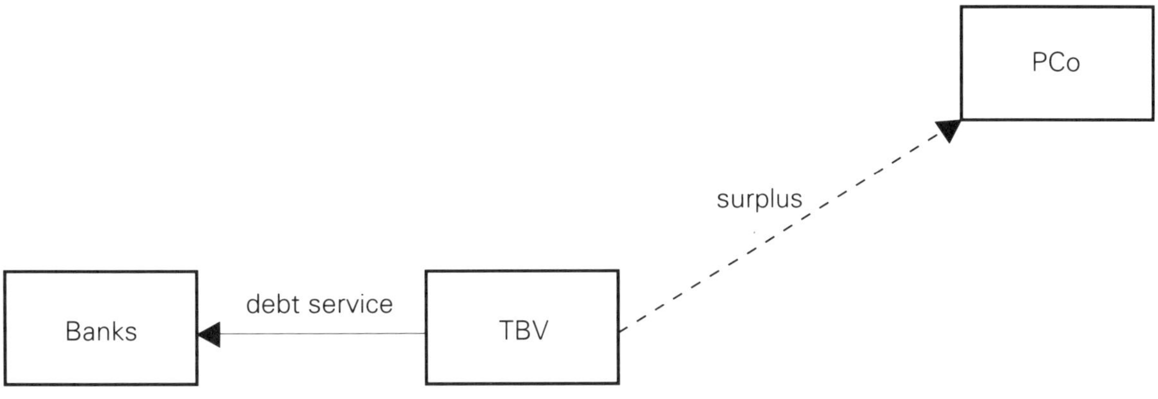

3. From the revenues, TBV pays debt service to banks, surplus to PCo.
4. PCo undertakes to pay to TBV an amount equal to debt service if, for any reason, its payment directions to off-taker are changed.

(d) The TBV structure

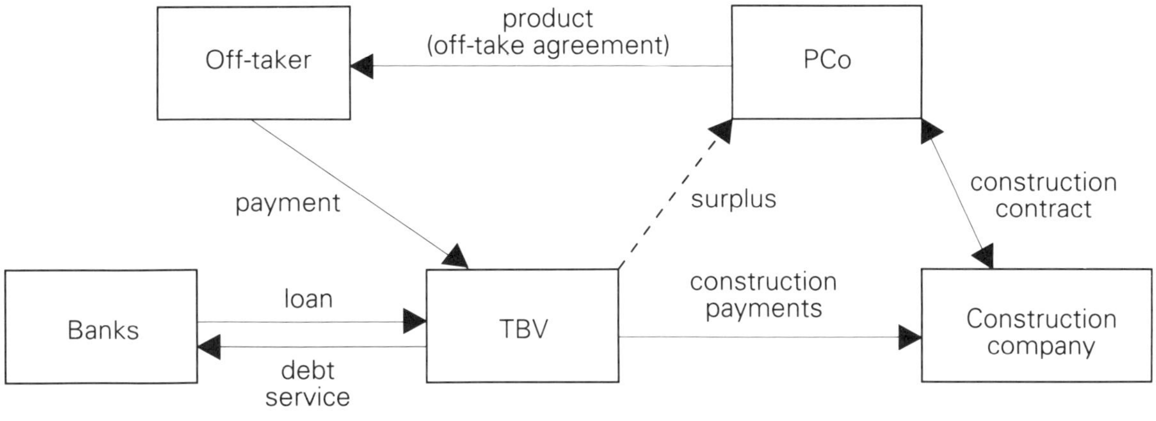

Thus, the structure can be represented as above.

(d) The banks

The sheer scale of many projects dictates that the financing will be syndicated. A syndicate of banks might be chosen from as wide a range of countries as possible to discourage the host government from taking action to expropriate or otherwise interfere with the project and thus jeopardise its economic relations with those countries.

The syndicate might well include some banks from the host country, particularly if there are restrictions on foreign banks taking security over project assets. *Pro rata* sharing agreements can be arranged so that security taken by the local banks is effectively pooled for all lenders. The total finance package for a project might involve different tiers of lending: some secured, some unsecured; some short term and trade-related, some long term; part of the finance might be subordinated to the rights of other lenders or creditors.

Commercial banks might also act as guarantors. For example, where concessional-rate financing is available from multilateral organisations or where export credit finance is involved, some or all of the commercial banks (who might also be providing direct loans to the project) might agree to issue guarantees or to open letters of credit in favour of the concessional-rate lenders. The benefits to the sponsors of obtaining the concessional finance on what is, in effect, a limited recourse basis (since the concessional lenders' risk is transferred to the commercial banks) could well outweigh the cost of paying guarantee fees and commissions.

From the perspective of the commercial banks, this arrangement has the advantage that they do not have to share the project security with the export credit lenders nor suffer their interference in accelerating the finance or enforcing security. This might justify the additional risk taken on under the guarantees, particularly if the concessional lenders would have required a first priority interest in the security proceeds in any event. Such a structure can be illustrated simply as shown in Figure 2.

Figure 2: A syndicate structure

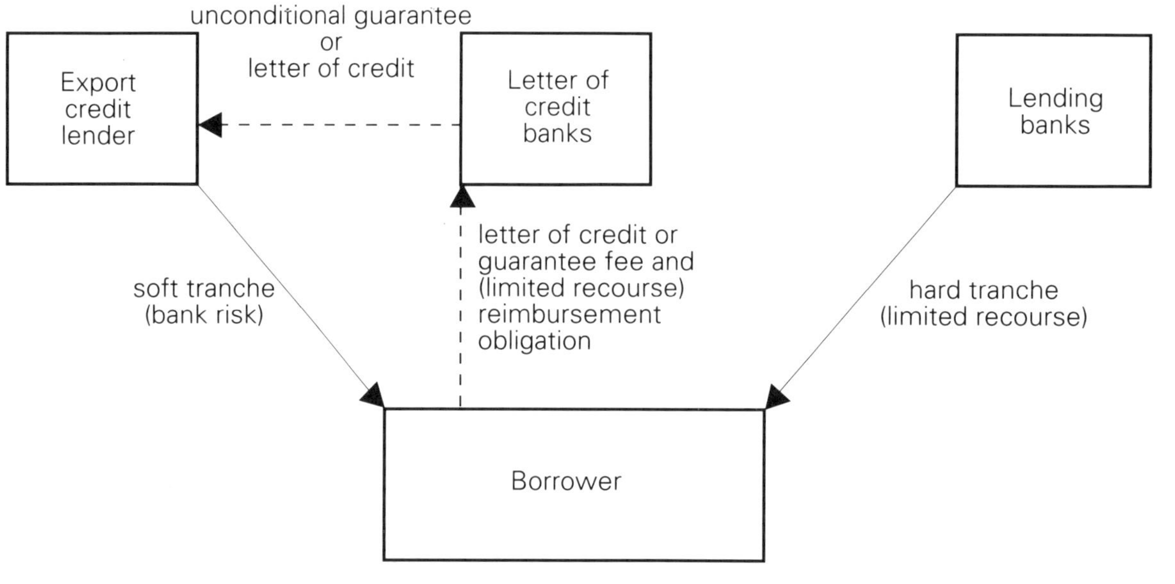

In some projects, commercial banks might find themselves acting as guarantors or depositors, standing behind "front" or "conduit" lenders whose loans are exempt from the withholding taxes that would apply if the commercial banks were to lend direct to the borrower.

(e) The arranger

The bank which has arranged the financing and syndication of the lending will normally take the lead role in negotiating the terms sheet and the credit and security documentation. The documentation will, however, contain explicit acknowledgements on the part of each lender in the syndicate that it has exercised its own judgment in entering into the transaction and that it will not seek to hold the arranger responsible for any losses suffered.

(f) The managers

Managers and lead managers might be named in the documentation and in any publicity surrounding the launch of the project. In most cases this status reflects a certain level of participation in the overall facility. The managers will not normally assume any particular responsibilities to the borrower or to the other lenders.

(g) The agent

The agent bank will be responsible for coordinating drawdowns and dealing with communications between the parties to the finance documentation, serving notices and disseminating information. The agent, like the arranger, will not be responsible for the credit decisions of the lenders in entering into the transaction.

(h) The engineering bank

Often, one (or possibly more than one) bank will be designated as the engineering bank, with responsibility for monitoring the technical progress and performance of the project and liaising with the project engineers and independent experts. The engineering bank might well be an affiliate of the agent or the arranger.

(i) The security trustee

In a straightforward project financing involving a syndicate of lenders, it is not uncommon for the security to be held by the agent bank in its capacity as security trustee. In some projects, however, there might be different groups of lenders or other creditors interested in the security and the coordination of their interests will call for the appointment of an independent trust company as security trustee.

(j) The financial adviser

In many cases, the project sponsor will retain the services of a commercial or merchant bank as financial adviser. The adviser will be familiar with the country where the project is located and can advise on structures and local conditions as well as having the expertise and contacts to "sell" the project to the lending banks. Indeed the financial adviser might be a lender too. The financial adviser will prepare, but seldom accept responsibility for, an information memorandum outlining the nature and economic feasibility of the project, setting out the relevant assumptions relating to project costs, market prices and demand, exchange rates and so on, together with a profile of each of the project sponsors.

(k) The experts

Selected by the project sponsors or by the financial adviser, technical experts of international repute might be retained to prepare, or at least vet, the feasibility study for the project. The expert will often have a continuing role in the monitoring of the progress of the project, possibly acting as the arbiter in the event of disagreements between the sponsors and the lenders over the satisfaction of the performance covenants and tests stipulated in the finance documents.

(l) The lawyers

The complexity of the documentation and the international make-up of the parties in large-scale project financing dictates the retention of experienced international law firms. Project sponsors will be well advised to conduct a review of the legal, tax and regulatory system in the host country as part of their preliminary assessment of the feasibility of the project. Local lawyers' opinions will be required as a pre-condition to lending from all relevant jurisdictions, including the home countries of the borrower and of the project sponsors and the place where the project assets are located, if security is to be taken over these assets. The lenders' legal counsel will usually be responsible for coordinating this advice. It is advisable to involve the lawyers at an early stage to ensure that the structure of the financing is properly conceived, to ensure that the necessary security arrangements can be put in place and to ensure that anticipated tax and other incentives or benefits are indeed available. Project sponsors, lenders and their legal counsel should not assume that ownership, tax or financing structures developed and tested in one jurisdiction will necessarily be appropriate in any other; the host country might well have a less sophisticated legal environment than that to which the parties are accustomed; or it might simply employ concepts that are fundamentally different, with their origins in the political, economic, cultural or even religious experience and beliefs of that society. The major international law firms can, perhaps, be expected to anticipate problems and to apply a flexible approach more readily than those whose experience is restricted to Western legal concepts and systems.

(m) International agencies

Many projects in developing countries are jointly financed by the World Bank or its private sector commercial lending arm, the International Finance Corporation, or by regional development agencies such as the Asian Development Bank. Projects in Central and Eastern Europe might have the support of the recently-established European Bank for Reconstruction and Development (EBRD). These agencies have their own policies and standards on issues such as security, termination of the financing and enforcement, which could influence the structure of a transaction. Projects tied to aid programmes or to other concessionary finance will invariably be structured to take into account the wishes of the agency providing the cheap funds. Simplified examples of structures involving such agencies are outlined in Chapter 3(8).

(n) The host government

In many cases the host government does not participate directly in a project finance as the borrower or as the owner of the project company, even in BOT (build-operate-transfer) infrastructure projects. However, host governments might take an equity interest through an agency and/or be the main off-taker of the product or user of the service to be provided and, in the case of a BOT arrangement, it will inherit the project at the end of the concession period.

Often the host government is involved less directly, but still in a crucial role, as the grantor of relevant concessions or operating licences, by making available incentives such as tax benefits or as guarantor of foreign exchange availability.

(o) Insurers

Proper insurance cover is a crucial aspect of project finance: security over insurance proceeds is an important safeguard, particularly when recourse to the borrower and/or sponsors is limited. The enormous scale of many projects and the potential for incurring all sorts of liabilities dictates that a close working relationship with the insurance brokers and underwriters is developed, to ensure that risks are correctly identified and covered. The availability — and price — of adequate cover for, say, environmental liability will vary according to the level of environmental protection provided for by the legal system of the host country.

(p) Leasing companies

If capital allowances are available for the writing-down of plant and machinery or other assets, the project structure might involve one or more financial leasing companies. Their role will be to acquire and lease out all or some of the assets to the project company in return for a rental stream calculated to both cover the acquisition cost and provide a commercial return.

(q) Rating agencies

Some projects might be financed by way of debt securities, backstopped by banks, either for tax reasons or to achieve finer rates. If the paper needs to be rated, the relevant rating agencies should be consulted at an early stage: their policies might have a bearing on the structure of the financing. In such cases, the ratings of the backstop banks will be critical.

(2) Feasibility study

Before any project can be "sold" to commercial lenders, its feasibility — technical and economic — must be presented in a convincing and authoritative manner; this will involve coordination of technical experts, financial and legal advisers and a thorough review of all aspects critical to the viability of the project. The checklist overleaf indicates some of the issues that will need to be considered.

Checklist: Feasibility study

The feasibility study should address:

- ❐ the extent and certainty of reserves — in extraction projects;
- ❐ the likely throughput — in pipeline or tolling (processing) projects;
- ❐ the likely passenger or traffic flows — in transport projects;
- ❐ the costs of acquiring the project site, construction and development;
- ❐ the availability and cost of services to the project site: energy, water, transportation and communications;
- ❐ access to supplies of raw materials, from either domestic or foreign sources; whether there are tariff or foreign exchange barriers to imports;
- ❐ the existence of accessible markets — domestic and/or foreign — for the product or service and the demand within those markets;
- ❐ the availability of necessary technology, equipment, management personnel and labour;
- ❐ the availability and transferability of operating licences and other official permits;
- ❐ projections of costs and returns, based on assumptions as to interest rates, exchange rates, inflation, taxes, delays and other contingencies;
- ❐ the existence of any potential for added value: eg, property development or by-product sales;
- ❐ the environmental impact of the project and the need to comply with environmental protection legislation;
- ❐ the availability and convertibility of currencies and the effect of foreign exchange controls; and
- ❐ the availability of insurance against project and country risks.

(3) Restrictions on borrowers/sponsors

The organisation and structure of a project finance might be affected by restrictions imposed on the borrower company or on one or more of the project sponsors by:

- its articles of association or equivalent constitutive documents or by the laws of its own jurisdiction;
- the restrictive covenants (pari passu clauses, borrowing limitations, negative pledges, cross-default clauses) applicable under its existing financial documentation or that of its affiliated companies; or
- the provisions of the joint venture agreement between it and its co-sponsors or licensing agreements with relevant authorities; these might take the form of pre-emption rights, negative pledges or commitments to withdrawal or abandonment of the project which are clearly inconsistent with the requirements of the lenders. Ways in which lenders might mitigate these problems are considered in Chapter 5(1).

(4) Restrictions on lenders

Project sponsors and their advisers should be aware that prospective lenders might be subject to restrictions which will not allow them to finance the project in the way that sponsors might expect:

- some banks are subject to restrictions on doing business other than banking, and cannot undertake commercial activity or maintain significant equity holdings in commercial enterprises;
- some jurisdictions might restrict the ability of foreign banks to acquire security interests;
- involvement beyond the basic banker-client relationship might give rise to a range of liabilities that banks are not prepared to accept, for example, owners' liabilities to third parties or for environmental damage;
- banks in certain countries might be subject to regulatory restrictions on participating in facilities involving specific country risk; and
- banks will have their own policies regarding customer, country and (possibly) business sector exposure.

Chapter 3: Project finance structures

(1) Types of finance

Whilst every project finance has its own special features, the basic structure is often either:

- a limited or non-recourse loan, repayable out of project cash flows; or
- a purchase of an interest in the project output (translated into sales proceeds) in consideration for the payment up-front of a capital sum either as a "forward purchase" or a "production payment".

In each case, "hell or high water" commitments on the part of suppliers, purchasers or users connected with the project might operate effectively to ensure that the lenders recover their capital and make a commercial return. Alternatively, lenders might be prepared to take the risk of repayment from the proceeds of production or user fees by relying on the open market.

In appropriate cases, these basic structures can be adapted to accommodate a number of other financing techniques, including:

- *lease financing*: in some circumstances leasing can be an attractive method of financing part, or even the whole, of the project cost, particularly in those jurisdictions where leasing permits the benefit of tax allowances for capital expenditure on the project to be front-ended (leasing structures are outlined in more detail in Chapter 3(6));
- *export credits*: where export credits are available, the basic financing structure can be adapted to accommodate the requirements of the relevant agencies; and
- *issues of securities*: in some cases it might be possible to provide finance at a lower all-in cost by the issue of securities (such as commercial paper), backed by commercial bank or other guarantees. Projects that are operating successfully might be able to raise funds through the issue of securities without the benefit of guarantess.

(2) Loan structures

The basic structure of a limited or non-recourse project loan is fairly conventional. If the borrowing entity is a limited liability vehicle established by the project sponsors, the documentation might not provide for any overt restriction on recourse, the lenders accepting that the repayment obligation is that of the vehicle, not of the shareholders. If the borrower is not merely a vehicle, then the limitation on recourse to the borrower and/or its assets will need to be dealt with in very clear terms.

For lenders, the advantage of dealing with a company that is not a vehicle is that all of its assets, perhaps even its other projects, might be available either to support the particular project that is being financed or to repay the lenders if that project runs into trouble. On the other hand, the documentation is likely to involve a certain amount of "ring-fencing" to protect those other assets. Moreover, the existence of negative pledges and other restrictive covenants imposed on the borrower by its other creditors might prevent the lenders exerting as much influence as they might like to. From an English law perspective, one advantage of financing a vehicle company is that the lenders are more likely to be in a position to take a floating charge over all the assets of the company. By doing so, they not only acquire a security interest in the assets but can prevent the appointment of an administrator (under the Insolvency Act 1986) that would otherwise seriously impair the lenders' ability to enforce their security.

(3) Project phases

Typically, the loan agreement will recognise at least two distinct stages in the project:

- the construction or development phase; and
- the operation phase.

During the first phase, the loan will be disbursed and debt service might be postponed, either by rolling-up interest, pending the generation of cash flows in the operation phase, or by allowing further drawdowns to finance interest payments prior to the operation phase.

The construction phase is the period of highest risk for lenders. It is not uncommon for the financing to be on a full-recourse basis at this stage, through legally binding guarantees of the project sponsors. Alternatively, margins might be higher than during other phases of the project. The risks will be mitigated by taking security over the construction contract and related performance bonds.

Recourse to the sponsors might fall away, or the higher margins might be lowered, upon the satisfactory completion of the project according to pre-set standards agreed between all parties in the documentation and verified by independent experts. Completion will mark the beginning of the operation phase when cash flows can be expected and the debt starts to be serviced and/or amortised.

In the operation phase, the lenders will take further security — over the sales proceeds or other revenues generated by the project. The rate of debt service and repayment will usually be related to the anticipated level of output and receivables of the project: a "dedicated percentage" of net cash flows will go to the lenders automatically. The terms of the loan will frequently provide for this to be increased — to anything up to 100% — in circumstances where output or demand for the product is lower than expected or where the lenders might have cause to feel uncertain about the prospects of the project, the sponsors or the surrounding economic or political climate.

Figure 1: Loan structures/project phases

(a) Construction phase

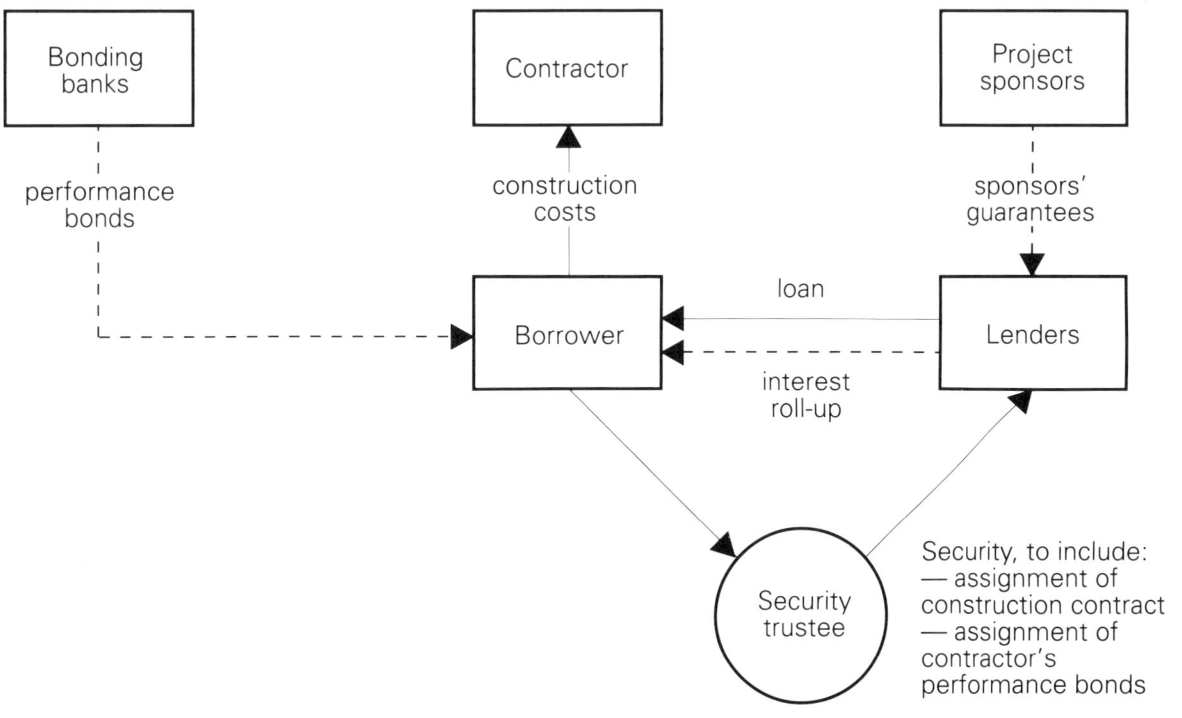

(b) Operation phase

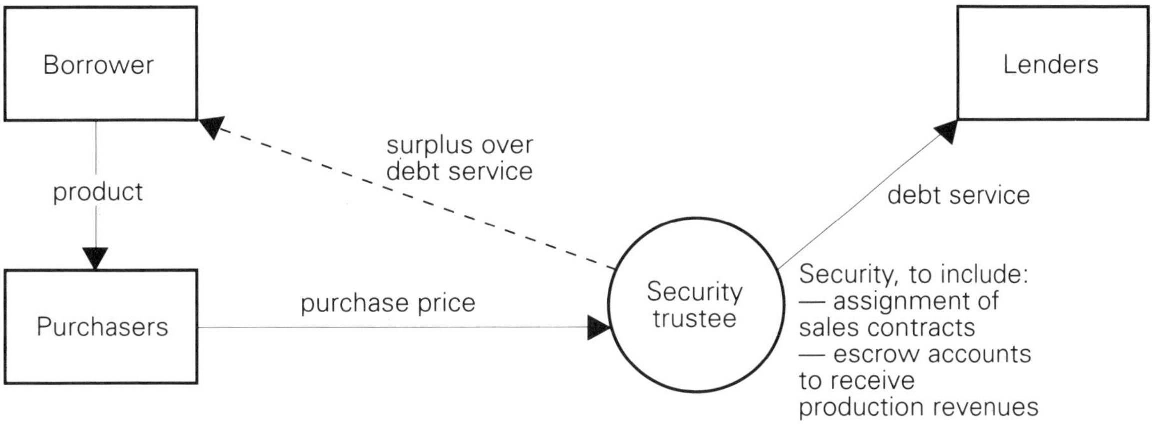

In the operation phase, net cash flows will more commonly be calculated on an after-tax basis. In some cases, there might be reasons why the project sponsors will wish to see net cash flows calculated on a pre-tax basis. If the lenders have made finance available against pre-tax cash flows, they will in effect be lending more than the net returns justify; in such a case the lenders will normally retain a degree of recourse to the borrower or guarantors for the tax "element", in the event of a default.

(4) Production payments

The production payment is most closely identified with US oil, gas and minerals project financing. It is an accepted method of achieving non, or limited, recourse financing with complete security (through ownership, rather than through assignment or mortgage) over the product and sales proceeds.

Briefly, the technique involves the establishment of a special purpose vehicle (SPV) to purchase an undivided interest in the oil, gas, minerals or other product from the project company. In some structures, the SPV will be established by the lenders.

The use of an SPV might help to isolate any potential liabilities (for example, environmental liabilities) arising out of ownership of the reserves or product.

The production payment structure is typically arranged so that:

- the exclusive source of "repayment" and "debt service" is the production of the project;
- the finance will be repaid over a period shorter than the anticipated economically viable productive life of the project; and
- the "lender" is not responsible for financing operating expenses of the project.

The viability of the structure depends, in part, on the ability to transfer title to the oil and gas reserves and associated rights and interests. This can be an important issue, for example, in the UK oil fields, where the pre-production rights of the oil companies are merely to operate the fields on the basis of licences, and ownership of oil in the ground remains vested in the state.

The lender might be entitled to all, or an agreed fraction, of the project's production until the debt is repaid, together with an interest element. In this structure, the repayment and debt service profile is determined by regarding the price paid by the lenders as the net present value (NPV) of future production proceeds.

The structure will usually oblige the project company to re-purchase the product delivered to the lenders or to sell it as agent for the lenders to realise cash. Sales might be anticipated as market sales or, more commonly, as sales under take-or-pay or similar "hell or high water" arrangements. The lenders do not expect to take actual delivery. The costs of the financing will include premiums for risk insurance taken out by the lenders for any liabilities arising out of their nominal ownership of the production.

A straightforward example of a production payment structure to develop a US oil field is shown in Figure 2.

Figure 2: Production payment structure

(a) Development phase

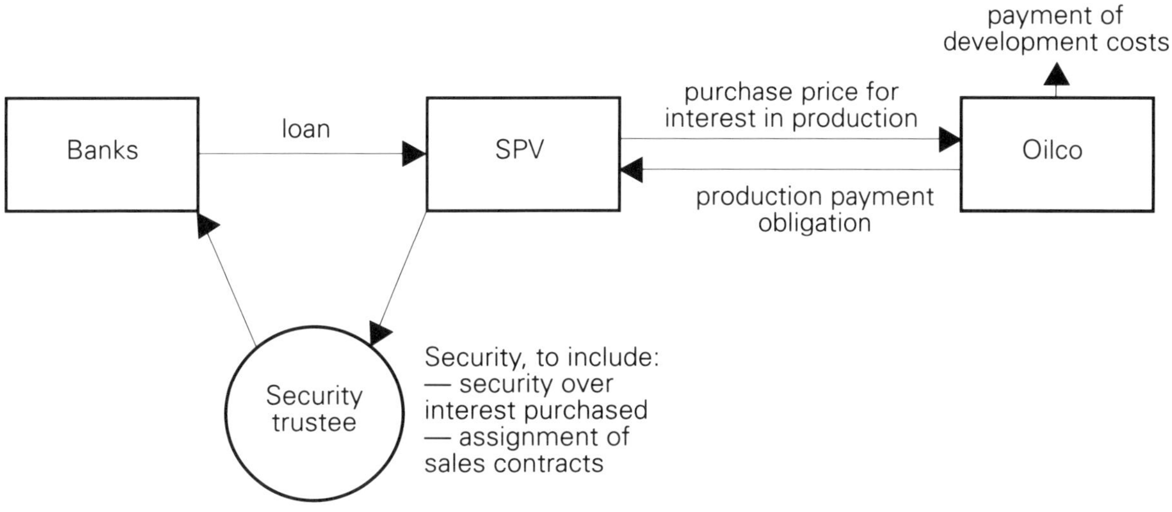

1. An SPV is incorporated. Banks lend to SPV the purchase price of the agreed interest in oil production from field owner (Oilco). Oilco agrees to make production payments calculated with reference to purchase price plus "interest" element, to be met from sale of oil. Oilco uses funds to pay development costs. Banks take security over SPV's interest and sales contracts.

(b) Operation phase

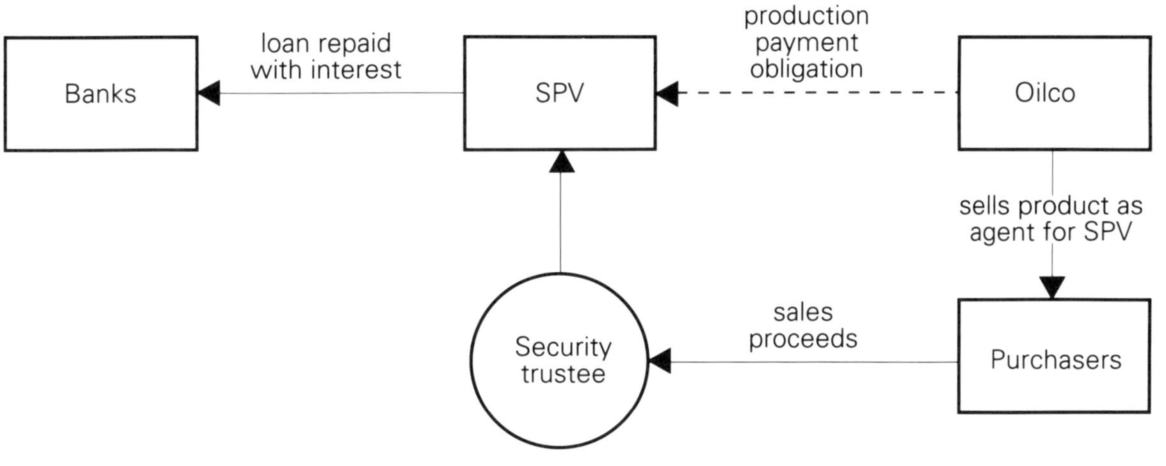

2. When production starts, Oilco sells production to purchasers as agent for SPV; proceeds used to discharge production payment obligations.

(5) Forward purchase

More flexible than the production payment, the forward purchase structure shares many of its characteristics. The lenders might set up an SPV to purchase agreed quantities of future production and/or the cash proceeds. The project company's obligation to deliver the product or proceeds will be formulated to match the agreed amortisation profile and to service the debt.

The purchase contract will normally require the project company either to buy-back the production or to sell it on to third parties as agent for the lenders, either in the open market or under take-or-pay or comparable arrangements with the sponsors.

As in the case of production payments, the lenders will take out insurance cover against risks attributable to their ownership, albeit momentary, of the product.

(6) Finance leases

The use of a leasing structure is extremely common in asset-based financing, particularly in ship and aircraft finance. A significant number of large-scale projects have also been financed using finance leases in jurisdictions such as the US and the UK, where the availability of substantial capital allowances on plant and machinery have been taken advantage of by project sponsors to achieve cost savings over a conventional borrowing structure.

There are signs in the UK of a revival of interest in the use of leasing structures, particularly in the context of a number of large-scale power generation projects that are under consideration. This level of interest confirms that, even though recent years have seen a significant reduction in the availability of capital allowances, the benefits that can be passed on (in the form of rentals that reflect the write-down claimed by the lessor) to project sponsors are sufficiently attractive to justify the greater complexity of documentation and associated legal costs and other fees.

Project sponsors and lenders might look to leasing for other reasons, not necessarily concerned with the opportunities for benefits from the tax treatment. For example, in financing the acquisition of assets in countries which have inadequate or uncertain security laws, the prospect of leasing — where the ownership of assets remains in the control of the lenders — might offer greater comfort. Short-term operating leases might find a place in a project financing structure, where the project company requires the use of specific assets only for a particular phase of construction or development.

Leasing, or techniques comparable to it, could have an increasing role to play in other areas; for example, in the development of techniques of Islamic finance which strive to generate returns for investors which are not derived from the charging of interest.

The essential structure of a finance lease for the financing of plant and machinery in the UK can be outlined as in Figure 3.

The documentation between the lessor and the guaranteeing banks will regulate the "acceleration" of the lease payments following "events of default" and the enforcement and realisation of security. Negotiating the coordination arrangements can be the most difficult part of putting together a lease-based project finance. The lessor will be concerned to retain its ownership interest and the right to repossess the assets under the lease to cover any potential loss that it foresees, notwithstanding the existence of the banks' guarantees. The banks will want to take effective security interests in the assets to cover their guarantee liabilities. Priorities between lessor and banks will always be a matter for negotiation but it is unlikely that the lessor will relinquish priority except, perhaps, in respect of indemnity claims — other than indemnities in relation to tax.

The scope of the banks' guarantees will be the subject of considerable negotiation, particularly if the lessor insists on cover for environmental liabilities that might arise as a result of its ownership interest during the period of the lease, which could well be as long as 20 or 30 years. Generally, banks will seek to restrict their guarantees to cover only rental payments and financial liabilities which can be specified. They will be reluctant (to say the least) to give blanket coverage for all of the indemnities given by the project company under the terms of the lease.

In large projects, the structure outlined in Figure 3 might be complicated by the fact that no one leasing institution has sufficient tax capacity to deal with the whole financing; assets might be acquired and leased separately by a group of leasing companies; alternatively they could hold the assets jointly through a partnership, although this has become less common in recent years. Where there is more than one lessor, it will not always be possible to vest in a particular lessor assets which both fit its investment limit and which give it an integral security which can be realised in isolation from the other assets spread among the group of lessors. In such cases, the coordination agreement will provide, essentially, that the whole plant shall be sold as a going concern in an enforcement situation. The procedures for effecting realisation of the assets and the basis of sharing the sales (or insurance) proceeds will have to be agreed to the satisfaction of each of the lessors involved.

Figure 3: Structure of a finance lease

(a) Contract stage

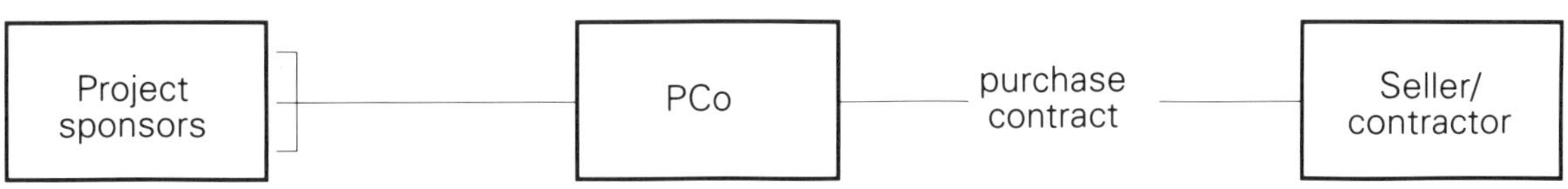

1. The project sponsors identify the plant and machinery that they wish to acquire and incorporate an SPV project company (PCo). PCo — or one of the sponsors — might enter into a contract for the purchase and construction of the assets which will subsequently be novated to a finance leasing company; alternatively, the contract will not be entered into until the finance leasing company has committed itself to the transaction.

(b) Lease stage

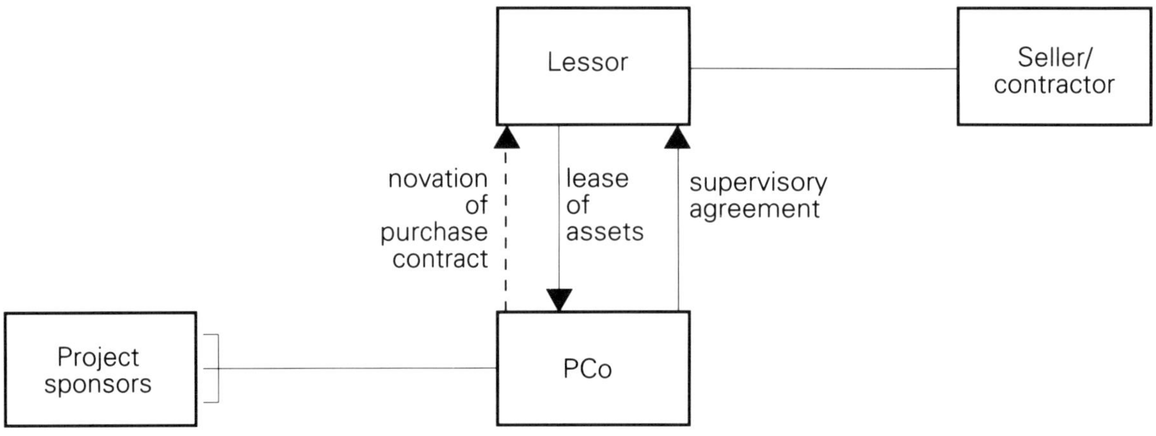

2. The finance leasing company leases the plant and machinery to PCo. The construction contract will be supervised by PCo (or it could be done by one of the project sponsors) on behalf of the lessor under a supervisory agreement.

(c) Construction phase

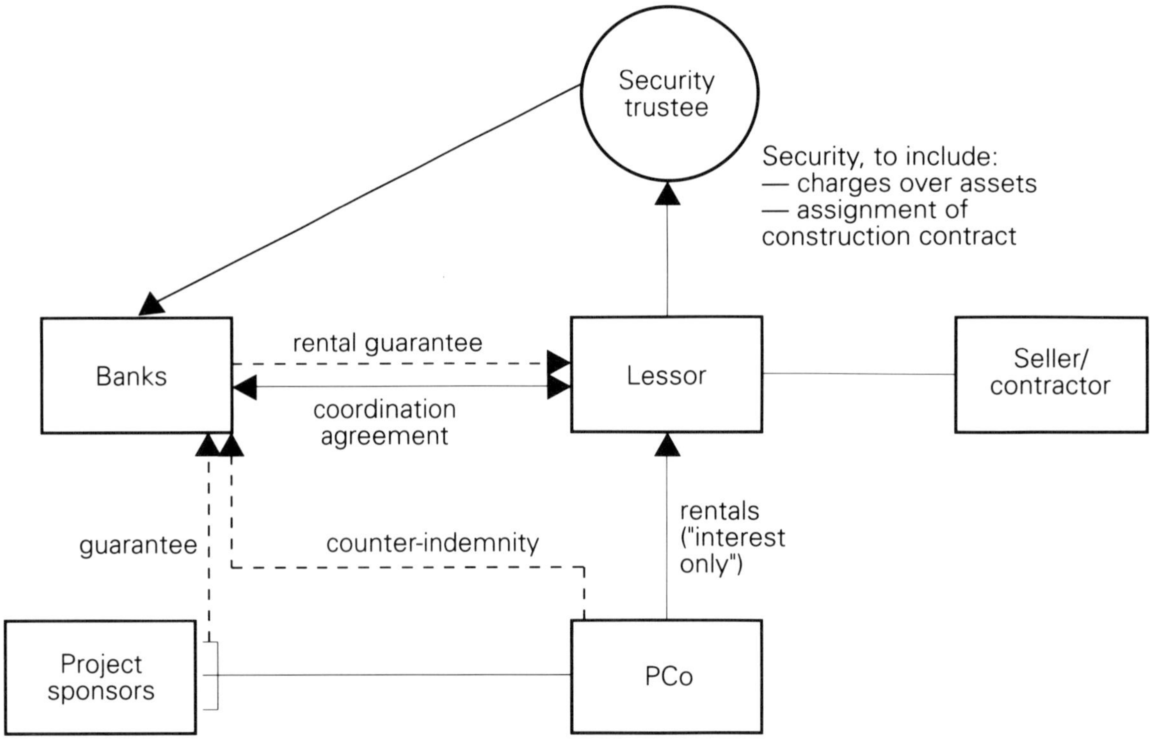

3. During the construction phase, rentals will be restricted to an amount equivalent to interest on the acquisition and construction costs. Rentals will be guaranteed by one or more banks or, less commonly, by the project sponsors. (Lessors will not, generally, accept project risk.)

4. The banks will take security from the lessor over the project assets and construction contract, subject to a coordination agreement with the lessor (as outlined above). During the construction phase, the banks might well require full or limited guarantees from one or more of the project sponsors to support PCo's counter-indemnity obligations.

(d) Operation phase

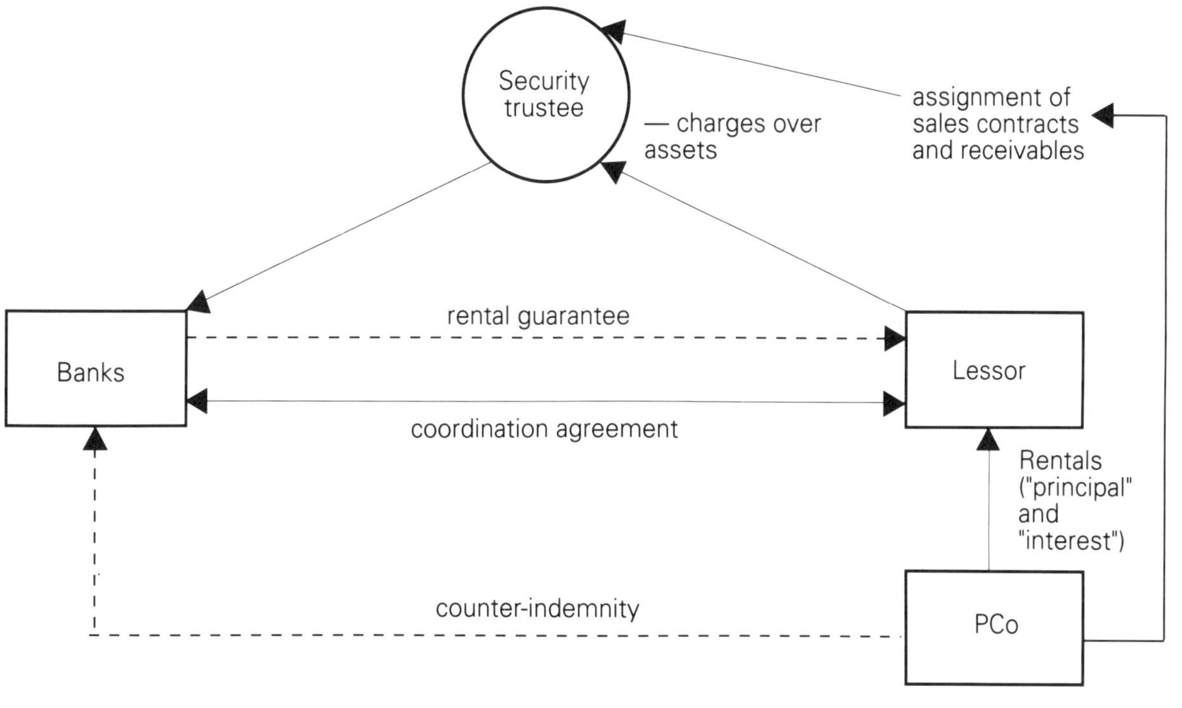

5. After completion, during the operation phase, the lease will provide for rentals to be reviewed to cover "principal plus interest" over the balance of the primary lease period. The sponsors' guarantees might drop away, leaving the banks with project risk, secured by assignments of the sales contracts and receivables as well as charges over the leased assets. The lease will set out completion tests comparable to those found in other forms of project finance documentation.

(e) Final phase — termination of lease

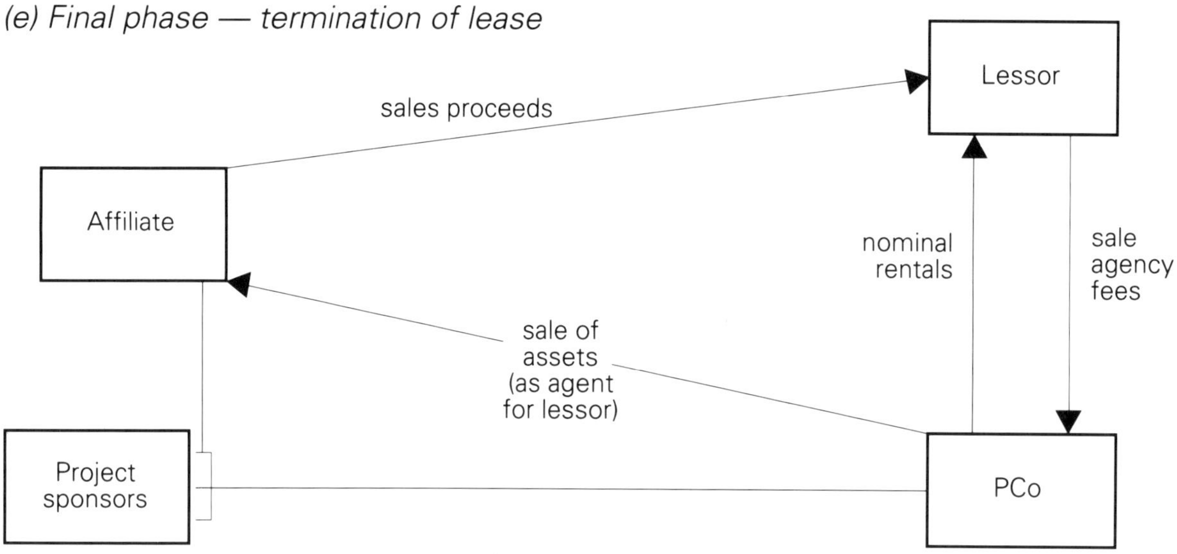

6. At the end of the primary period, when the lessor's costs have been paid off, and the lessor has achieved the desired commercial return, the lease will normally continue for secondary or tertiary periods of substantial length, at minimal rentals. The lease will not contain a purchase option exercisable by PCo — otherwise this would characterise the transaction as hire purchase and eliminate the tax benefits attaching to the structure. The lease might well provide that PCo shall act as sole agent to sell the assets at the end of the term at a price acceptable to the lessor; the bulk of the sale price will be refunded to PCo as sale agency fees. It is quite possible that the purchaser would not be unconnected to one or more of the project sponsors.

(7) Build-operate-transfer (BOT)

The structure known as BOT is sometimes regarded as a type of privatisation, but this analysis might be somewhat misleading. Except where the concession period approaches the project's useful life expectancy, an essential element of the BOT structure is the transfer back of the operational project to the relevant state authority. It is therefore perhaps better to think of a BOT structure as a method of turning over to the private sector, for a limited period, the development and initial operation of what would otherwise be a public sector project.

The BOT approach is likely to be particularly attractive to a government that is keen:

- to minimise the impact on its capital budget, thus enabling it to implement a project at a time when it could not itself provide the requisite funds or, alternatively, leaving it free to use its resources for other schemes which might be of less interest to the private sector; and/or
- to introduce increased efficiency from the private sector; and/or
- in developing countries, to encourage foreign investment and the introduction of new technology.

A BOT structure is normally based on a concession agreement between a government, or a government agency, and the vehicle company established by the sponsors to carry out the construction and operation of the project. This is not invariably the case, however, and in an early application of this structure in China, the Shajiao B Power Station (described in more detail in Chapter 8(5)), the concession was effectively granted through a Chinese cooperative joint venture contract between the responsible Chinese enterprise and the foreign investment vehicle.

In addition, where the liabilities undertaken by the project vehicle are substantial and the vehicle itself has been incorporated specifically to obtain the concession, the sponsors might themselves be required to provide support for the vehicle's performance, whether by entering into the concession agreement or providing independent commitments. Conversely, the sponsors will wish to ensure that the government party accepts that it might, in certain circumstances, need to provide continuing support. For example, connecting infrastructure might need to be put into place and payments might need to be made for the benefits received from the project once it becomes operational. In projects where the product or service supplied is primarily of a social nature — for example, transportation or energy projects — BOT might be a particularly appropriate structure.

Sponsors are likely to require assurances as to a government's intentions on a range of further issues which might affect the project. While governments are unlikely to be either willing or able to fetter the future exercise of their legislative and administrative powers, sponsors might nonetheless try to ensure that adequate compensation shall be payable in the event that the government subsequently acts inconsistently with its expressed intentions and to the detriment of the project.

Looking further at a BOT structure from a government's point of view, it will be concerned to ensure that, for example:

- the concession company provides an adequate service throughout the term of the concession;
- the concession company observes relevant safety and environmental protection standards;
- the charges levied upon consumers are reasonable; and
- proper works of maintenance and repair are carried out in order to provide an adequate service, to meet necessary safety and other requirements and to ensure that, on transfer at the end of the term, the government inherits an operational project and not simply a liability.

There might be different ways for a government to achieve such objectives ranging from specific regulatory enactments to the maintenance of a "golden share" in the concession company.

It is vital to the financing of a BOT project that the role of the lenders is recognised and accommodated. The concession agreement itself is likely to effect a substantial degree of the project risk allocation and negotiations between the relevant parties on these issues should take account of the likely response of lenders to this allocation of risk. In addition, in BOT projects the host government not only plays a much greater role than in other projects, but also might have little direct contact with the lenders. Since the interests of the host government and the lenders will not necessarily coincide, it is essential for the sponsors and their advisers fully to appreciate the particular requirements of all parties involved.

An example of a BOT structure is shown in Figure 4.

Figure 4: A BOT structure

(a) Concession

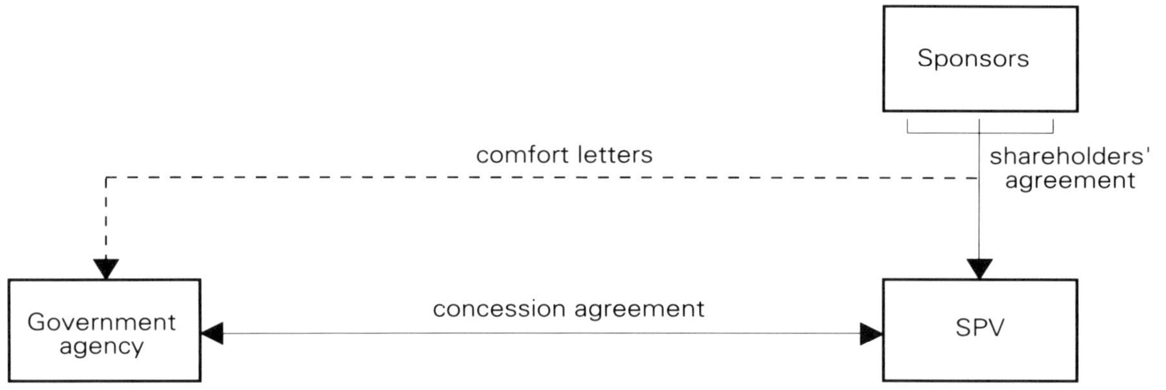

1. Sponsors incorporate SPV to undertake concession agreement; shareholders enter into letters of comfort with government agency.

(b) Construction

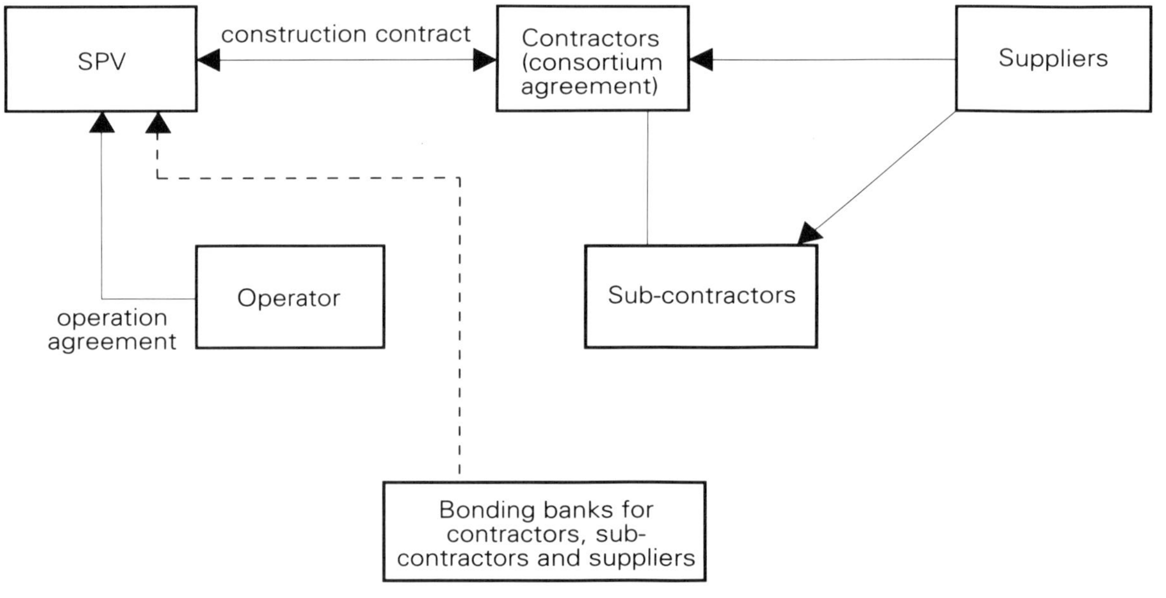

2. SPV enters into construction contract, takes bonds and assignment of sub-contractors'/suppliers' bonds; enters into operation agreement.

(c) Finance

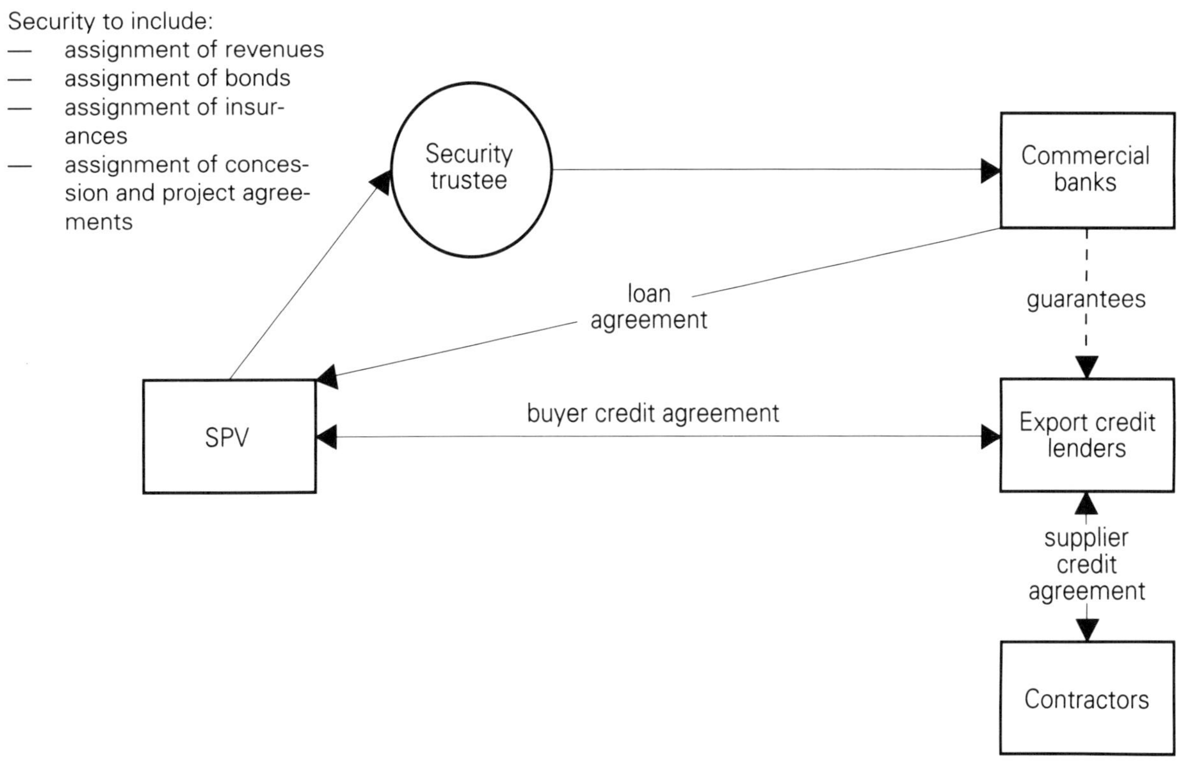

3. SPV enters into loan agreement with commercial banks and buyer credit agreements with export credit lenders; commercial banks guarantee export credit loans and take project security.

(d) Operation

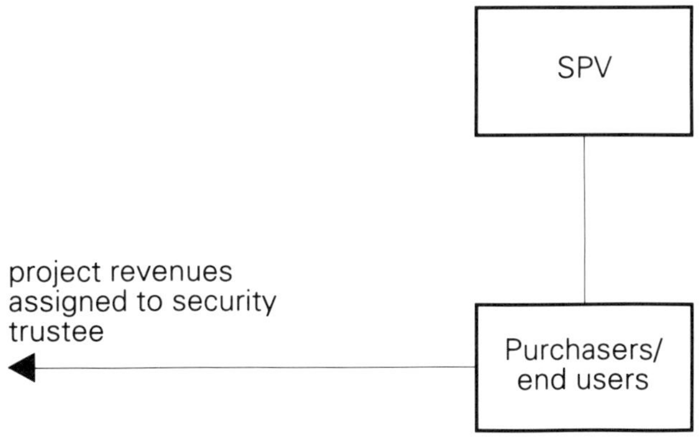

4. SPV assigns revenues (eg, proceeds under sales contracts or toll fees for a road, tunnel or bridge) to security trustee.

(e) Overall structure

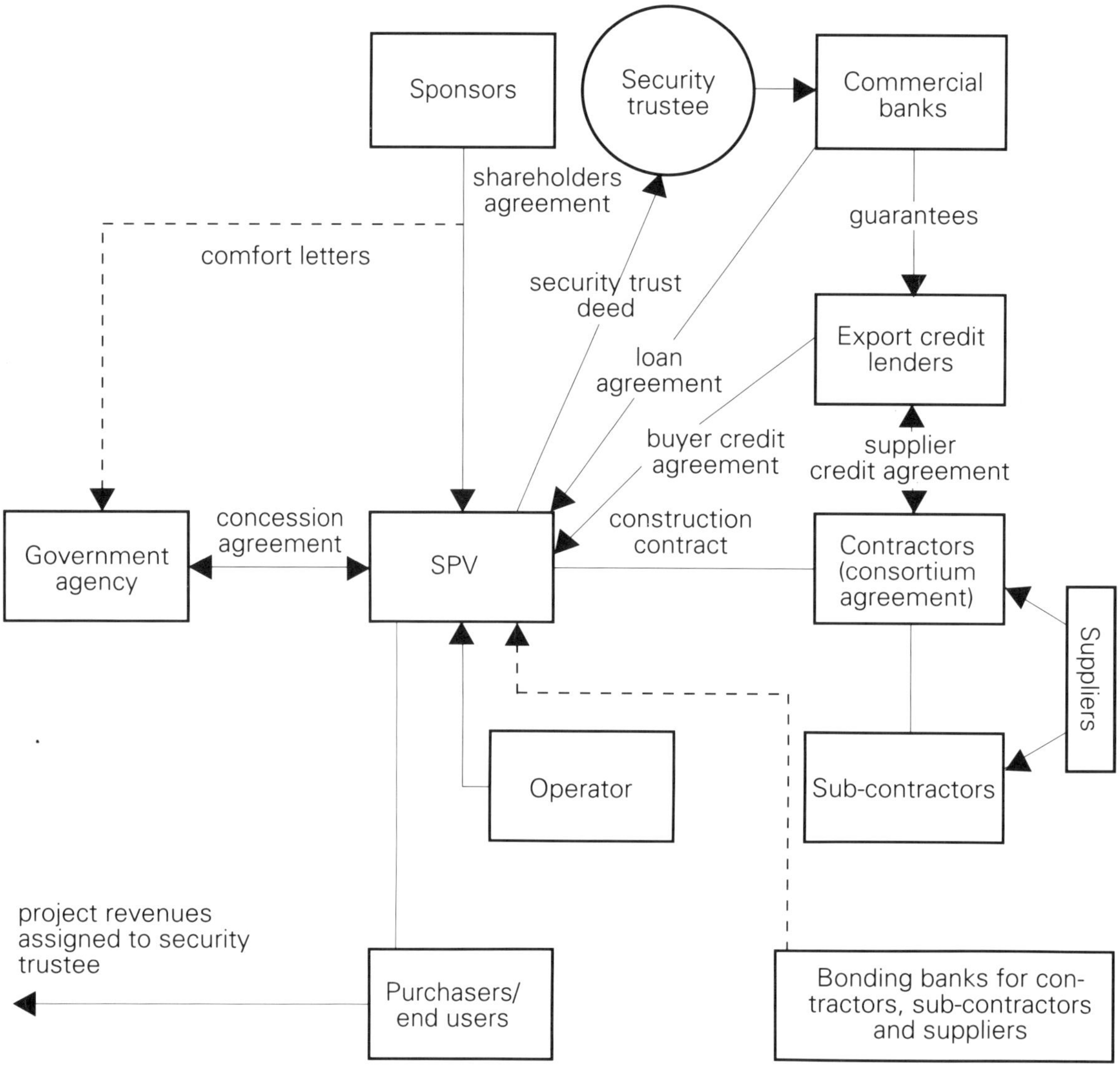

The overall structure can thus be represented as shown above.

(8) Project financing with the World Bank and other multilateral institutions

Many projects, particularly those carried out in developing countries, are co-financed by multilateral agencies. For project sponsors based outside the host country, the involvement of, say, the World Bank or its private sector lending arm, the International Finance Corporation (IFC), might alleviate some of the concerns about the political risks that might be involved in doing business in that country. Lenders, too, might feel that the prospects of the repercussions that the host country would face — were it to interfere with the interests of the parties involved in a co-financing structure — operate in practice as something of a deterrent, though there is of course no legal basis for this.

In public sector projects supported by the World Bank, finance might be made available at concessional rates. State guarantees will always be required by the World Bank if it is not actually lending to the government.

By contrast, the IFC lends to the private sector and seeks no state support. Its rates are not concessionary: indeed margins might be high, indicating that many of the IFC's borrowers would struggle to raise funds from commercial banks at rates available to other borrowers. The high margins and the political risk "comfort" associated with IFC financings can attract commercial lenders into co-financing projects that otherwise might not get off the ground.

The types of projects that are financed by the IFC are designed to benefit the host country's economy, usually by increasing its hard currency earning capacity, compatible with structural adjustment policies that might have been implemented there under World Bank or IMF supervision. The borrowers will be locally incorporated enterprises, but these might well have 100% foreign participation, if local laws permit that.

Project appraisals are subject to ever-stricter environmental impact assessments: problems and delays might be encountered in complying with other policy requirements, such as the World Bank's guidelines on competitive bidding for contracts and economy and efficiency standards.

A simplified example of an IFC co-financing is demonstrated in Figure 5.

Figure 5: An IFC co-financing structure

(a) Project structure

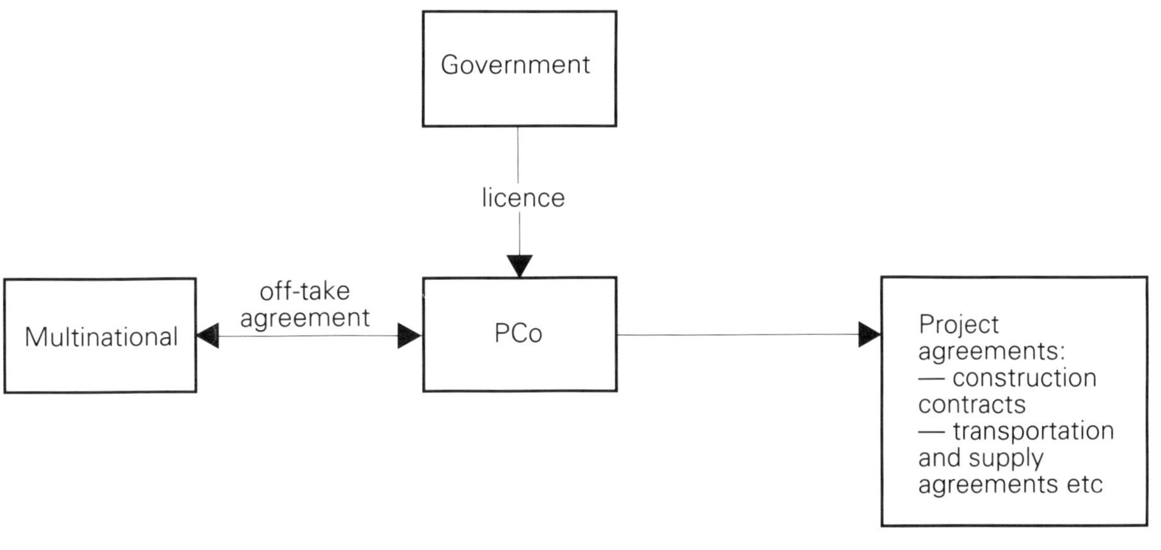

1. Multinational mining company establishes local subsidiary (PCo) to exploit mineral/metal deposits in developing country; PCo obtains government licence, enters into project agreements and into an off-take agreement with its parent.

(b) Finance

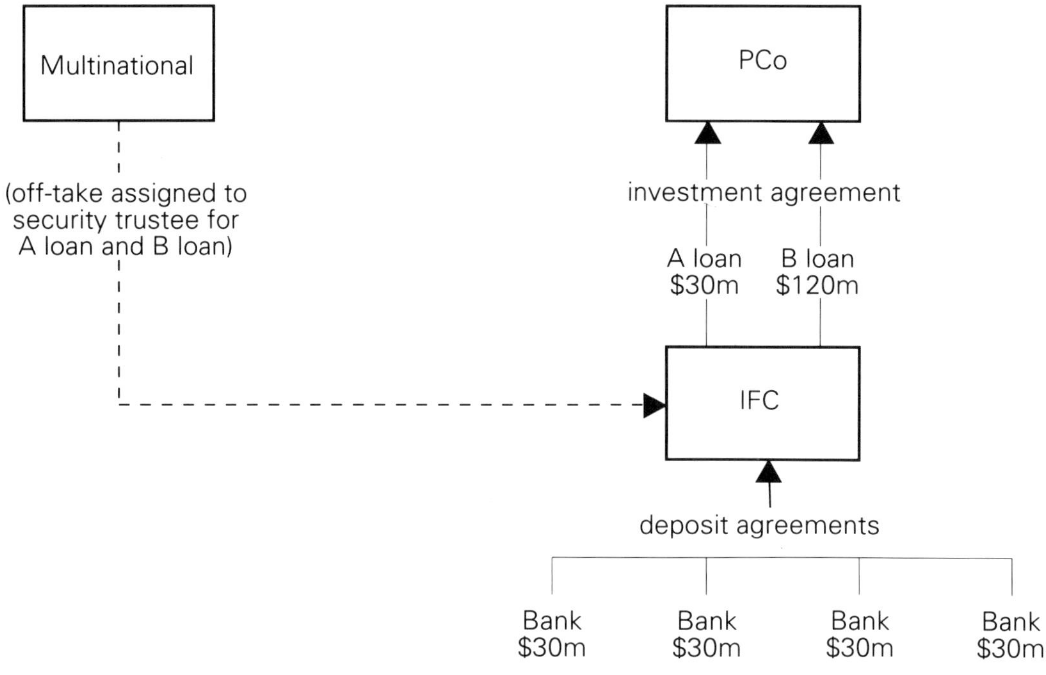

2. IFC enters into "investment agreement" with PCo, for US$150m and makes separate "deposit agreements" (on a participation basis) with commercial banks for 80% of the total loan.

3. The structure involves no direct contractual relationship between the banks and the borrower. Under the documentation, IFC retains control of covenant performance, acceleration and payments; there is no formal agency structure as there would be in a conventional syndicated loan agreement.

Co-financings between commercial banks and the World Bank, or a regional development bank, of loans to a state or state entity might be structured differently. The loans will probably be syndicated in a relatively conventional manner; the state will give guarantees to the World Bank and, with second "priority", to the commercial banks.

The World Bank is unlikely to require security for its own account but will impose a strict negative pledge on the borrower and will usually wish to share the benefit of any security taken by the commercial banks. If such security is granted, the coordination provisions of the documentation will usually permit enforcement by the banks only with the World Bank's approval. A simple example can be represented as in Figure 6.

The documentation will usually contain a specific provision that excludes any inference either that the World Bank, IFC or other co-financing agency is acting in the capacity of a government of any state.

The commercial banks will be required specifically to acknowledge that they have entered into the transaction exercising their own credit judgments and without reliance on the decisions taken by the co-financing agency; any responsibility or duty on the part of the agency to the commercial banks is excluded, except for those responsibilities that are explicitly set out in the documentation.

Figure 6: World Bank co-financing

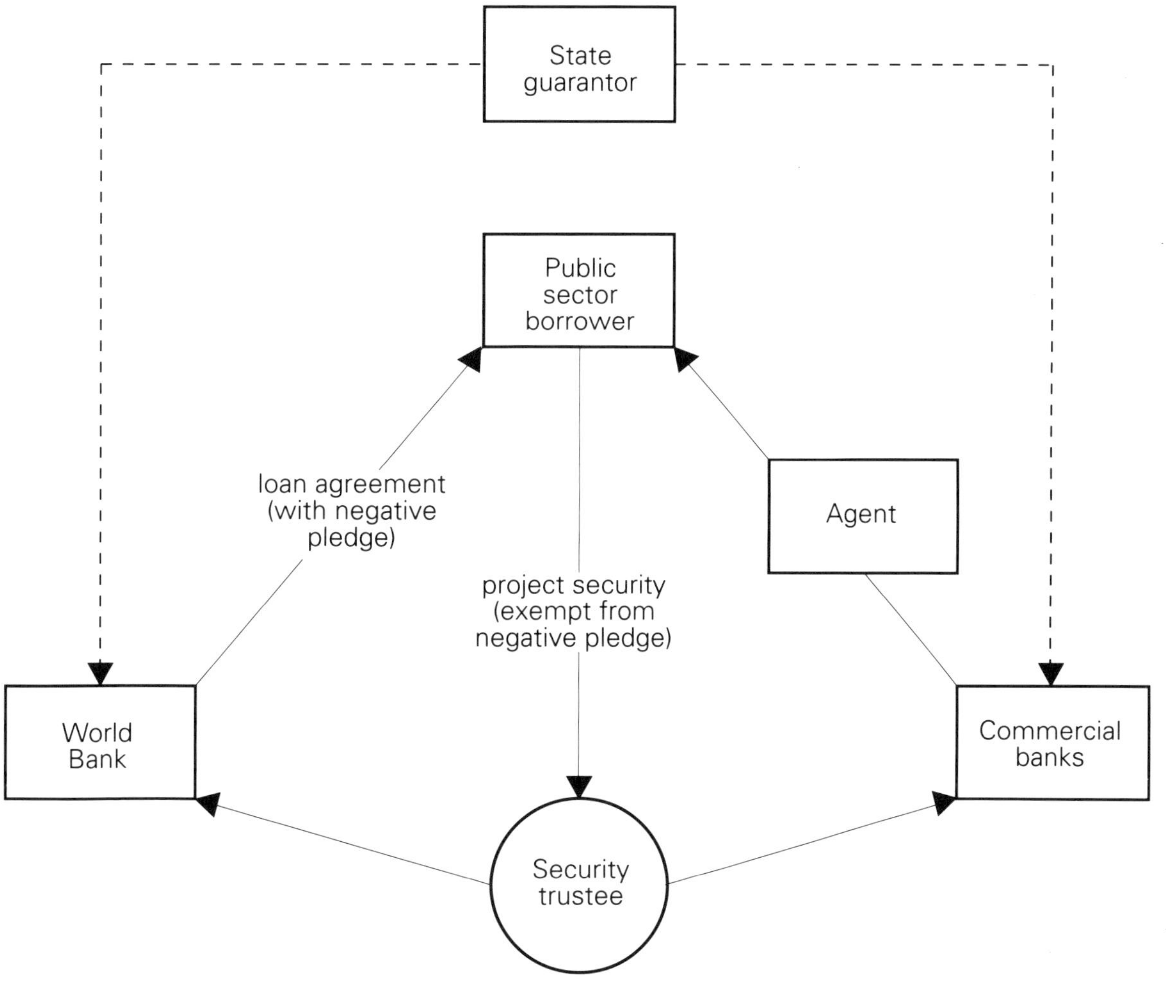

(9) North Sea oil financing — an illustration of structures and problems

One established area for project finance is the financing of North Sea oil fields. The following summary of what might, cautiously, be described as a "typical" project will illustrate some elements of a limited recourse financing structure; it will also highlight that, even in a sector such as this, some important problem areas remain unresolved.

The structure can be outlined as in Figure 7.

Figure 7: North Sea oil finance

(a) Licence

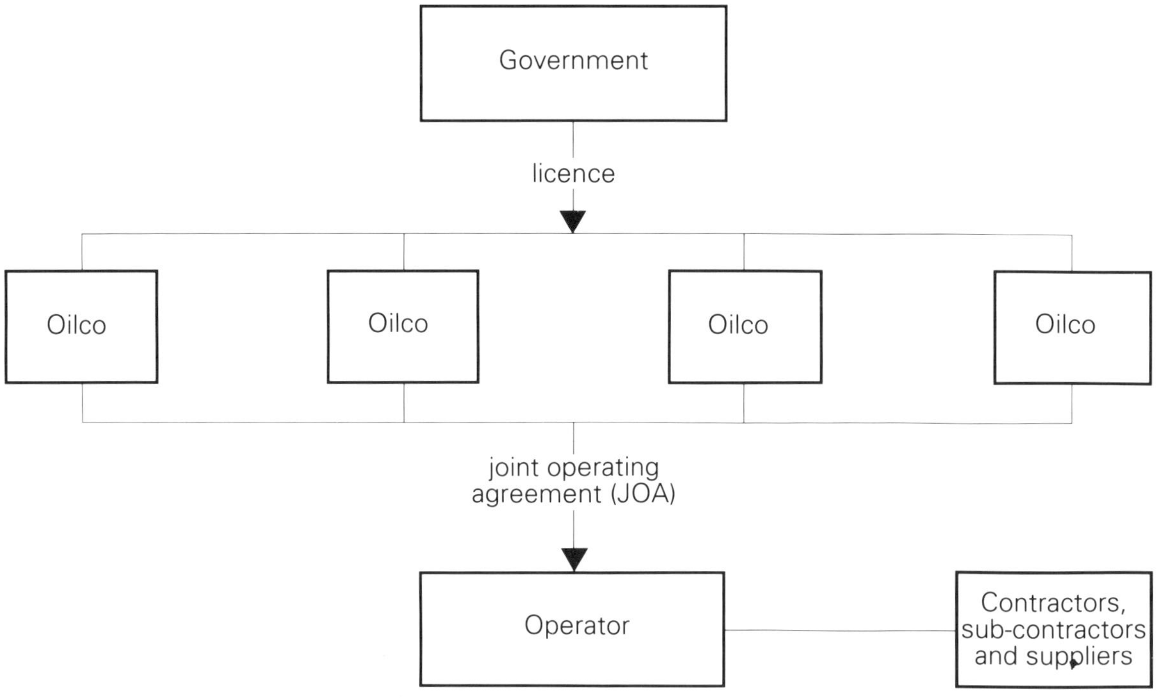

1. Development and operation of a North Sea field will typically be the joint effort of a number of major oil companies. Their roles and responsibilities will be coordinated by a joint operating agreement (JOA) which will nominate one company to be the field operator. The operator will enter into contracts for building rigs and staffing and will generally be responsible for undertaking the work of the project. The JOA will determine each company's entitlement to the joint venture assets, including petroleum lifted from the field under the licence. The JOA will also set out the voting rights and procedures for decision-making and for setting budgets and funding the different stages of development and operation through cash calls made by the operator.

2. Royalties will be paid to the government which has granted the licence; property in the petroleum will only vest in the oil companies once it has been lifted; so long as it remains in the ground, it is the property of the state.

3. Each oil company will, typically, make its own arrangements for disposal of its share of lifted petroleum. It is interesting to contrast the position in a gas project where it is likely that the JOA will contain detailed provisions about off-take and pipeline arrangements, having regard to the more restricted markets for disposal of the product.

(b) Finance

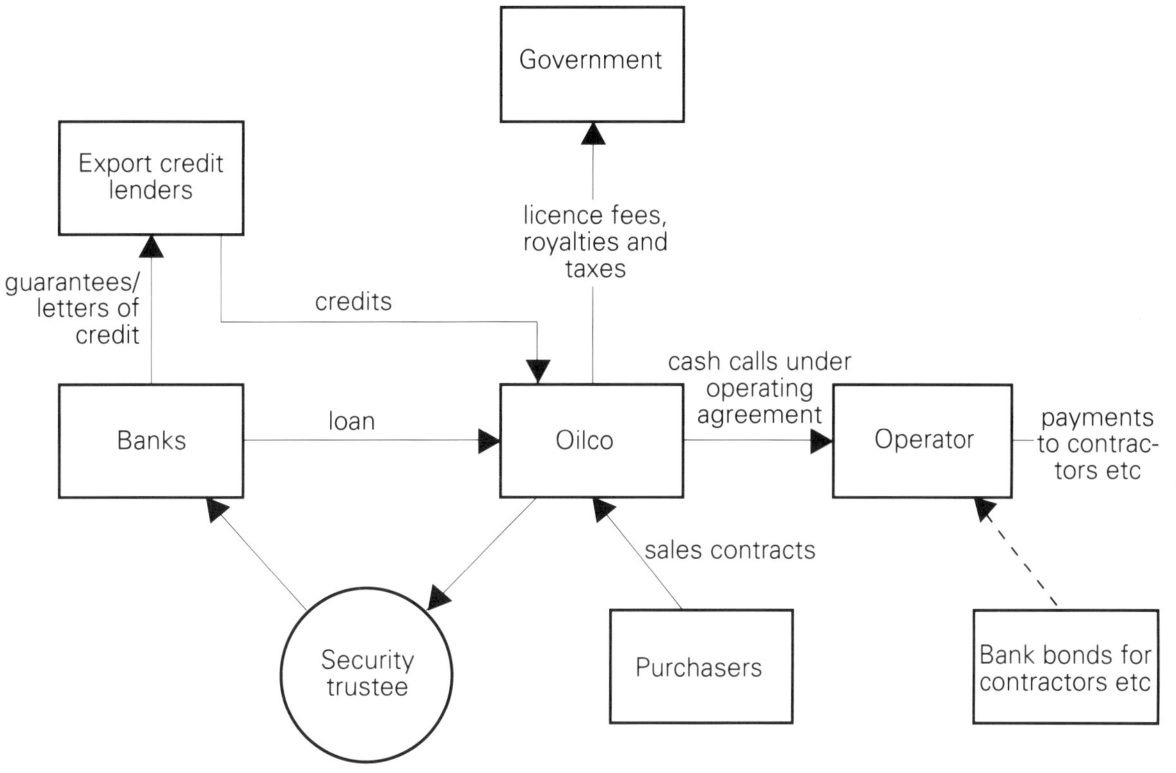

4. Each oil company participating in the project will make its own arrangements for funding cash calls made by the operator. It is not usual for finance to be coordinated for the entire field development. Some companies might raise funds on a corporate basis, others by borrowing on a limited recourse basis. In the case of borrowing, it will usually be necessary to create security, which will typically include:

- a mortgage over the company's share in the licence (the consent of the state licensor will be required);
- a charge over the company's interest in the JOA;
- a mortgage over the physical assets in the field;
- security over the oil in the pipelines or to which the company is entitled (in the UK by way of a floating charge and in Norway by way of an "inventory mortgage");
- an assignment of sales contracts and sales proceeds in escrow accounts;
- assignments of project agreements and transportation agreements; and
- assignments of insurances.

Unless an SPV has been incorporated for the project, it is unlikely that lenders will be granted floating charges over all the assets of the borrower.

5. If there are different tiers of lenders, for example, export credit lenders as well as commercial banks, the banks could avoid the need for complicated and possibly unsatisfactory security sharing arrangements by issuing letters of credit or guarantees to the export credit lenders, effectively giving them bank risk and giving the banks unhindered access to the project security.

One potential problem area in the context of security is the fact that government consent to the creation of a mortgage over an oil company's share in an operating licence does not guarantee that the banks will be able to enforce that security. In the case of the UK government, the licence will provide that a further consent will be needed if and when the banks wish to enforce. The position is similar in the case of Norwegian consents. In recent years, the UK government has become increasingly reluctant to give any "comfort" that the second consent will be a mere formality. Licences issued by the UK government provide that the very act of enforcement, that is, the appointment of a receiver by the lenders, can of itself constitute grounds for revocation of the licence. Despite the potential problems banks have, in practice, shown themselves willing to rely on these governments being cooperative.

The form and nature of the security that can be taken over the field facilities will depend in part on the geographical location of the field: within the UK continental shelf areas, English and Scottish security techniques might be required. In many cases, both are put into place for "belt and braces" protection. Norwegian security law methods will have to be applied in Norwegian territory. New security laws have been developed in Norway in response to concerns that the legal framework did not offer adequate protection to project lenders.

The degree of recourse to the borrower and/or its parent company will vary from case to case and will depend on whether the borrower is an SPV or a more substantial UK company with other projects. In the case of a loan to a more substantial company which will not permit the lenders to take a floating charge over all of its assets, the lenders are vulnerable to the appointment of an administrator who can effectively hinder attempts by the lenders to enforce their security.

Other problems connected with enforcement might arise from the terms of the JOA itself. The circumstances affecting the borrower which have given rise to the problem could of themselves constitute events which trigger pre-emption rights or "withering provisions" — whereby the interest of any joint venturer who fails to meet a cash call can be "frozen" and, as development of the project continues, effectively taken up by the other companies. In some cases, the defaulting company might have to forfeit its interest, with no compensation. It is crucial, therefore, that banks should scrutinise the JOA before committing to fund the borrower and, in the event that such conditions apply, they should take pains to obtain waivers or other commitments of cooperation from its joint venturers.

Lenders to the defaulting company will be in a dilemma — should they put up extra funds to meet the cash call or should they risk losing what security they have for disbursements already made?

Lenders to the non-defaulting companies will also be forced to consider whether they will fund the additional costs of taking up the defaulting party's share in the project. To some extent, lenders might find themselves taking a credit risk on the other joint venturers.

Another circumstance in which licensees (and their financial backers) might be required to put up additional funds is where a new discovery is found in the same licence area. The JOA might well provide that, once a participant has committed itself to the development of a new discovery, it will have to fund its share of the development costs or risk forfeiting its interests under the JOA and/or the licence. Failure by the borrower to meet its commitments in respect of the development of the new field might therefore jeopardise the position of the lenders *vis-à-vis* the field that they are financing, even though — in respect of that field — the borrower is fully in compliance with its obligations.

Chapter 4: Project risks

(1) Credit risk

Even though project finance usually involves some concession on recourse to the borrower and/or project sponsors, lenders will still assess the creditworthiness, track record and management skills of the parties that they rely on to ensure the success of the project, namely:

- *the borrower and any guarantors* — if guarantees or other cash deficiency arrangements are available during the project's construction and development phase or thereafter;
- *contractors* — if some level of bonding is required to secure payment of liquidated damages for failure to perform;
- *the project sponsors* — if they have a key role in managing the project or if equity is to be injected or other support provided;
- *product purchasers* — if take-or-pay, take-and-pay or similar arrangements or other medium to long-term sales contracts are in place;
- *project suppliers* — if put-or-pay or other medium to long-term supply contracts are the anticipated source of raw materials;
- *project operators* — if the project is of a nature requiring advanced technical operation skills;
- *project users* — for example, in pipelines, where throughput or tolling agreements are in place;
- *other participants in the project* — where the interest of the project sponsors being financed is less than 100% of the project; and
- *insurers, re-insurers and insurance brokers* — for their ability to pay under the insurance policies and brokers' undertakings which make up the insurance arrangements.

The reliability, expertise and creditworthiness of these various parties are matters that concern the project sponsors no less than they do the banks that are financing the project.

(2) Construction and development risk

The lenders' assessment of risks in the construction and development phase of the project will involve careful scrutiny of the methodology and assumptions used in the feasibility study. Lenders will have to assess the likelihood and implications of:

- *shortfalls in the expected mineral reserves* — if the reserves of oil, gas or minerals prove to be less than the exploration surveys indicated;
- *shortfalls in expected capacity, output or efficiency* — if performance does not achieve plant rated output or anticipated efficiency (either because of defects in the engineering, design or technology or because the raw material is contaminated in ways that were not foreseen, for example, dangerous impurities in gold ore which complicate the refining process);
- *cost overruns* — in supplies and transportation of energy and/or machinery and equipment and/or raw materials or in the cost of contractors and labour;
- *delays in completion* — involving additional interest expense and lengthening of repayment profile;
- *availability of land, building materials, energy, raw materials and transportation* — for supplies to the project and for movement of products to market;
- *availability of work force, management personnel and reliable contractors*; and
- *force majeure* — force majeure risks are particularly acute during the construction and development phase of a project, but also apply during the operating phase. "Force majeure" essentially refers to factors outside the control of the parties, such as natural disasters — fire, flood, earthquake — and war, revolution and strikes, affecting the project itself or affecting contractors, suppliers or markets for the product.

Some of these risks can be minimised through:

- ensuring that the project company has entered into binding and enforceable long-term fixed price contracts for supplies, energy and transportation with creditworthy and reliable counterparties;
- the project establishing its own supply sources and connecting infrastructure, for example, by setting up transportation networks or power generating plants specifically for the project;

- requiring that performance bonds and completion guarantees are given on behalf of suppliers, contractors and sub-contractors and assigned on to the lenders;
- taking out commercial insurance and securing export credit guarantee support; and
- incorporating strict provisions in the underlying documentation, for example, with contractors and suppliers, to penalise delay and to fix costs and performance and efficiency criteria — the benefit of which may be passed on to the lenders by assignment.

(3) Market and operating risk

The feasibility study will also assess the risks associated with the operating phase of the project, such as:

- the existence of a local or international market for the product;
- the likely strength of any competition and any similar projects being contemplated; projections for world prices for the product; applicable tariffs and trade barriers;
- access to markets, both in terms of physical access (transportation and communications) and in terms of commercial access (whether potential purchasers are free to buy the product, or whether markets are controlled by central planning authorities);
- obsolescence — is the project going to produce products or a service that will still be wanted by the time it goes into the operating phase? There is a risk that the technology used in the project might be superseded; and
- new technology — as a rule, lenders are reluctant to support projects that use untried technology, for fear of delays, cost overruns and outright failure; this has to be weighed against the risk of being overtaken by more innovative competitors.

Long-term take-or-pay contracts (in manufacturing or resource extraction projects), throughput agreements (in pipelines) or tolling agreements (in processing plants) can minimise the operating risk by guaranteeing a market for the product at a price tailored to cover operating expenses and to service and retire the debt. In the case of electricity generation projects, there will often be only one possible consumer: a national or local grid. In such cases it is usual for the relevant utility agency to provide undertakings as to minimum off-take and price or, alternatively, to agree an availability fee arrangement (capacity charge) with further fees then payable for power produced.

(4) Financial risk

The project sponsors' financial advisers and the lenders should ensure that the feasibility study addresses the potential impact on the project of financial developments outside the control of the project sponsors, such as:

- fluctuations in exchange rates;
- increases in interest rates;
- increases in world commodity prices, especially for energy supplies and raw materials;
- falls in the price of the product on world markets;
- inflation; and
- trends in international trade, protectionism and tariffs.

These risks can be addressed in various ways in the finance package:

- the package can include hedging facilities against exchange rate and interest rate risks by way of currency and/or interest rate swaps, interest rate caps, collars and floors and other techniques;
- the debt service and repayment profile can be formulated by reference to a matrix of factors including market prices, inflation rates, energy costs, tax rates and so on as influencing the "dedicated percentage" of revenues allocated to the lenders or as determining the obligations of the project sponsors under the take-or-pay contracts, throughput agreements or tolling agreements that might be in place; and
- the package can include protection against a fall in the price of the product through hedging facilities such as forward sales and futures and options contracts, but sometimes at the risk of creating an additional financing requirement for margin calls.

(5) Political risk

In any cross-border financing, borrowers and lenders take a "political" risk in the sense that a collapse of the existing political order in the borrower's country or the imposition of new taxes, exchange transfer restrictions, nationalisation or other laws might jeopardise the success of the venture, the security of the investment and the prospects of repayment and recovery. In project financing, the political risks are more acute because:

- the project itself might require governmental concessions, licences or permits to be in place and maintained, particularly where the project is for power generation, transport infrastructure or the exploitation of the country's natural resources;

- ❒ the project might be crucial to the country's infrastructure or security and accordingly be more vulnerable to the threat of expropriation or requisition — power projects, airports, seaports, roads, railways, bridges and tunnels are obvious examples;
- ❒ the project might be of importance to the host government's social policies or to its international prestige, where considerations other than purely economic factors might be relevant, as in the case of the construction of hospitals, universities, sports stadia, hotels and other tourist facilities;
- ❒ the host government might impose additional tariffs on imports of plant and machinery or materials crucial to the manufacturing process of the project; domestic supplies might be insufficient or sub-standard; in some cases the whole purpose of the project might be to provide a facility for processing the (imported) materials of the (foreign) project sponsors;
- ❒ tariffs or, in situations of domestic shortages, quotas or prohibitions might be imposed on exports of the project's production;
- ❒ the host government might introduce controls to restrict the rate of production or depletion of the project's reserves, either for national reasons to do with the management of the host government's economy or for international reasons such as compliance with OPEC quotas;
- ❒ additional taxes might be imposed on the project's production, such as the surcharge taxes imposed by the United Kingdom on revenues from North Sea oil production;
- ❒ taxes or other restrictions might be imposed on repatriation of profits and debt service;
- ❒ the introduction of more stringent environmental protection legislation during the life of the project could adversely affect planned production rates or operating costs;
- ❒ the government might have pre-emption rights to purchase the production from the project in certain circumstances;
- ❒ the success of a project might well depend on the anticipation of changes in the political and economic culture of the host country — as in the case of many of the new projects being mooted in Central and Eastern Europe — which cannot be guaranteed to occur at the right time, or at all;

- in countries whose economies are organised under a "command" system, or which retain some elements of such systems, access to supplies of energy and raw materials and to markets, both domestic and abroad, might be restricted; a processing or manufacturing project will clearly require both; and

- conversely, a project might be planned on the assumption that fixed prices and regulation of access to markets will continue; "deregulation" or the lifting of tariff barriers might be detrimental to its prospects.

Political risks might be mitigated in a number of ways:

- licences granted to the project sponsors should be checked and clarified with the issuing authorities if they are ambiguous; perhaps the lenders' interest can be noted in some way to ensure that they are advised in advance of any proposal to modify, renew or revoke the licence; lenders might seek commitments to enable the licence to be transferred to them — or their nominees — in the event of the failure of the project company;

- assurances against expropriation or nationalisation might be sought, with guarantees that proper compensation will be payable in that event;

- central bank undertakings to ensure the continuing availability of foreign exchange should be obtained, if possible;

- if the project generates "hard" currency, for example, through sales contracts, it might be possible for the lenders to collect, control and, if necessary, retain the cash flows offshore;

- project sponsors — and lenders — should familiarise themselves with the tax and tariff laws of the host country and structure the project and its financing in such a way as to take advantage of double taxation treaties and bilateral or international trade agreements; project sponsors might be tempted to resort to devices such as transfer pricing to avoid taxation or exchange transfer restrictions; and

- insurance against political risks might be taken out either on a commercial basis or with official bodies, such as export credit departments or multilateral development agencies. This aspect is addressed more fully in Chapter 6(9).

More subtle ways of minimising the political risk might present themselves, depending on the nature of the project: if the financing is arranged in parallel with organisations such as regional development banks, the World Bank or aid agencies, a formal coordination of the lending structure might reduce the risk that the host government will interfere with the lenders' interests. Similarly, if the financing is syndicated to lenders from a wide range of "friendly" countries, the risk of jeopardising trade and other relations with those countries might deter the host government from taking action that is detrimental to the interests of the lenders or, indeed, the project sponsors.

(6) Legal risk

Many projects are carried out in developing countries where the legal system is less sophisticated than in the industrialised nations of North America and Western Europe. Others might be carried out in countries where the existence of a fundamentally different economic system has rendered it unnecessary for the legal system to provide many of the standard protections that exist elsewhere. For example:

- laws on the taking and enforcement of security, particularly in the case of moveable assets, cash flows and contractual rights (such as receivables) might be less than satisfactory, and existing laws might preclude the ownership of real property; in a project finance — particularly where recourse is limited — the ability to take effective security can assume crucial importance;
- protection of intellectual property rights — patents, trademarks, copyright — might be rudimentary or non-existent, or might not have kept pace with technological developments, such as in the field of computer software;
- the regulation of fair trading and competition might be inadequate; in countries with a recent history of command economies there might have been little reason for the legal system to address these issues;
- the concept of a trust might not be recognised; this could create problems for security sharing and transferability of lenders' interests;
- dispute resolution could be problematic; foreign parties might not have equal access to the courts; choice of foreign law might not be recognised; foreign judgments might not be enforceable; the ability to refer disputes to arbitration — sometimes the preferred method of resolving disputes over technical matters between the commercial parties (though not generally accepted by lenders) — might be restricted; and the status and enforceability of arbitration awards might be uncertain or unsatisfactory; and
- the local lawyers and the judiciary might be unversed in the sorts of issues likely to arise in project-related disputes; the legal system might be slower, more expensive and less predictable than lenders are accustomed to; rights of appeal might be limited and enforcement against assets located in the host country, particularly assets which become important to the national economy or security, could be problematic.

It is crucial for project lenders to undertake a thorough review of the legal risks at an early stage by taking the advice of their own local lawyers and, if possible, by seeking confirmation of the position from the host government's own law agencies — the ministry of justice, attorney general's office or equivalent. In some cases it might be necessary to pre-condition the financing on a change in the law itself — by requesting the passage of new legislation, possibly legislation which is particular to the project. Clearly, the likelihood of achieving this will depend on the size, nature and importance of the project to the local economy.

(7) Environmental risk

Growing public concern about the adverse effect of industrial processes and practices on the natural environment and on the health and well-being of the people living and working in it has led many countries to enact increasingly tough legislation controlling emissions, waste, the transportation of hazardous substances and inefficient use of energy and non-renewable resources. International conventions and treaties such as the Montreal Protocol on ozone layer depletion and proposals for conventions dealing with climate change, biodiversity and forestry reflect the concern of the international community to deal with environmental problems that have a global dimension.

Increasing acceptance of the "polluter pays principle" might lead to the development of a business, regulatory and accounting culture in which the environmental costs of industrial activities will be fully internalised within those industries that use natural resources and/or create pollution and will be, ultimately, passed on to the consumers of their products and services. In the short term, compliance with environmental protection legislation will involve substantial costs to industry but in the longer term it might lead to greater efficiency and the development of innovative techniques and new products and technologies which could give the "cleanest" and "greenest" businesses a competitive edge.

The costs of failing to comply with environmental legislation can be substantial. In the first major prosecution brought by the UK's National Rivers Authority, Shell UK was fined a total of £1m for its pollution of the River Mersey.

The potential costs do not simply arise from fines imposed on proven polluters. Indeed, the total cost to Shell UK of the Mersey incident is said to have been over £7m, taking into account clean-up costs, settlement of third party claims and installation of new systems. Some of the costs implicit in many aspects of current and proposed environmental regulation are indicated in the checklist opposite.

Environmental liabilities attach primarily to the project operators and, indirectly, to the project sponsors and lenders. Greater costs to project operators clearly can impact on a lender's assessment of the likely profitability of a project. But that is not the only consideration that lenders should bear in mind. Since project finance usually involves lenders in taking mortgages and other security over the project site and assets, lenders must be aware that if they exercise their rights under the security to take over the project, then they might well assume direct responsibility for the environmental impact of the project and its products.

If land associated with a project is contaminated, its value might be reduced and significant costs might be incurred in clean-up before the project is allowed to proceed. This could have a detrimental effect on the cash flows and viability of the project as well as on the realisable value of the lenders' security over the project site.

In the UK, the Environmental Protection Act of 1990 is a significant move towards integration of pollution control. The Act introduces a system of centralised control in respect of all discharges to the environment. Previously, each environmental medium — air, land and water — had been subject to separate rules and controls. The UK government has also recently (July 1991) announced proposals to establish a single environmental protection agency to enforce pollution controls. Many of the concepts reflect policies developed at the European Community level, particularly through DGXI (part of the EC Commission), which is behind many of the proposals to harmonise environmental standards, practices and procedures throughout the Community. The adoption of an EC Directive providing for joint and several strict liability for waste is expected in the near future, as is the establishment of a permanent home for the new European Environment Agency.

Checklist: Environmental costs

In addition to fines and penalties for pollution, environmental costs could include:

- ❒ fees payable to regulatory and licensing bodies;
- ❒ the cost of preparing environmental impact assessments to obtain planning permission for major projects;
- ❒ the cost of taking out insurance to cover the risk of environmental damage and compliance with associated risk management techniques required by insurers;
- ❒ the cost of compliance with new packaging and labelling requirements;
- ❒ the implementation of strategies for good environmental management and practice, eg, through environmental audit programmes;
- ❒ the cost of using best available technology or techniques not entailing excessive cost (BATNEEC) to prevent or minimise pollution from industrial processes;
- ❒ loss of profits arising from forced shut-downs of plant;
- ❒ clean-up costs of polluted sites and civil liabilities for damage to property, health or the environment;
- ❒ loss of value due to contamination of land;
- ❒ increased waste disposal, handling and transportation costs; and
- ❒ the imposition of environmental taxes on the use of non-renewable resources or the production of polluting products (note, for example, the incentives created by the differential taxes imposed in the UK on leaded and unleaded petrol respectively).

In North America, the legislative response to environmental concerns began much earlier and it is not unreasonable to look to the US for ideas as to how concepts that are now being employed for the first time in Europe might be developed. The Comprehensive Environmental Response Compensation and Liability Act 1980 (CERCLA) — also known as the Superfund Law — and the Superfund Amendments and Re-Authorisation Act 1986 create the US regulatory framework. Recent interpretations of these laws have given potential project lenders much food for thought.

The Superfund Law provides exemptions from liability for financial institutions whose "ownership" interests exist purely for the purposes of securing their loans. However, banks have been found liable as "owners" where they have gone into possession (even just for the purposes of a sale) or as "operators" if they have participated in the day-to-day management of the debtor's business. In a case in 1990, a bank was found to be liable where the extent of its involvement was to participate in the financial management of the debtor "to a degree indicating a capacity to influence" the company's treatment of hazardous waste.

In response to lobbying from bankers and fearing fundamental changes to the principles of liability enshrined in the Superfund Law, the US Environmental Protection Agency (EPA) itself released, in June 1991, a proposed legislative rule to clarify the lender's exemption. The new rule, if adopted, would establish that lenders must actively participate in management of a facility — and not just have the power to do so — before they lose their exemption. The exemption should apply to foreclosure on bad debts and activities such as monitoring and advising on the borrower's business and financial condition. Loan "work-outs" that involve some further limiting of the borrower's discretion should also be within the scope of the exemption.

The proposal suggests two types of participation that would not be exempt: where the lender has undertaken responsibility for hazardous waste activities that cause a contaminating release; and where the lender has been involved in the borrower's management at a sufficiently high level to include responsibility for day-to-day environmental compliance.

Since project finance frequently involves the imposition of strict covenants on the conduct of business — for example, the control of cash flow through special accounts, the conferring of veto powers on decisions such as abandonment of the project, alteration of project development plans, changes in transportation and supply arrangements — there is obviously some scope for lenders to be regarded as playing a role in the management of the project. The fact that banks are generally perceived to have "deep pockets" cannot be ignored in anticipating a willingness on the part of legislators, local authorities and courts to find a reason to attach responsibility to them for the cleaning up of major environmental problems.

How can project lenders protect themselves? Some general suggestions are:

❐ to become familiar with the legal framework governing environmental liability in the host country as part of the general assessment of the project's feasibility;

❐ to evaluate the risk of environmental liability associated with the borrower, the project site, the supplies to and transportation from the site, and the products, emissions and waste that the project will generate;

- lenders should ensure they have experts to evaluate the information that is gathered;
- satisfaction with the environmental position should be a specific condition precedent to making finance available, including ensuring that plans for the project allow enough tolerance for future tightening of environmental controls;
- documentation should contain representations, warranties and covenants on the borrower's part to ensure that the borrower focuses on these issues and complies with all applicable regulations and recommended practices; and
- on-going monitoring of the project should include environmental assessments, prepared on a basis that reflects intervening changes in environmental legislation.

Both project sponsors and lenders can attempt to reduce the risks by seeking insurance cover. However, insurance cover might be hard to come by for risks or costs other than those associated with "accidents". Cover might well not be available for loss that results from past pollution, gradual pollution or breaches of statutory duties. Fines and awards of damages will not be recoverable. Insurance cover, if available at all, will be limited in amount whereas the potential liabilities for major environmental damage are unlimited.

(8) Lender liability

In some respects, the potential liabilities for environmental costs that lenders face can be regarded as an example of "lender liability". The concept of lender liability is well developed in the US although it is still, comparatively, in its infancy in the UK. The fundamental principle behind the development of the concept in the US is that lenders must act in good faith and deal with their customers fairly.

One aspect of lender liability which is analogous to the problems considered in the environmental context is the exercise of "undue control" by a lender intervening in the customer's business by taking actions associated with ownership or management. Undue control can make the lender liable for the consequences if the borrower becomes insolvent. The need to draw a fine line between unacceptable "control" and careful credit monitoring is particularly acute in the context of project finance: the restrictions imposed on the borrower's operations, the reporting and monitoring of progress, the control of disbursements and receivables, and the insistence on comprehensive security packages, increase the likelihood that the lender might be regarded as having an active role in the conduct of the business.

The consequences of being held to have exercised "undue control" might go beyond the obligation to compensate the borrower for loss suffered. In some cases in the US, the courts have held that the degree of interference warranted that the lender be treated, *de facto*, as a partner in the business — with joint and several liability for its obligations to creditors.

The exercise of "undue control" is only one aspect of lender liability. US banks have been held responsible for the financial consequences of failing to make loans after entering into a commitment to lend. If a lender were to insist on terms being included in the loan documentation that were not addressed in the original offer, then this might be construed as a failure to negotiate in good faith. Once the documentation is signed, the lender might find itself responsible for failing to lend even where the facility was expressed to be uncommitted. A duty to act in good faith could be interpreted to mean that a lender must have a valid reason not to make an advance when requested.

A duty of good faith has also been implied in the US in the context of the exercise of the right to accelerate a loan upon default. It has been held that a loan can only be accelerated for a "material" default and that, where previous defaults have been tolerated, it was wrong to accelerate on the basis of a further default of the same type.

In project finance documentation, the list of conditions precedent that need to be satisfied before advances may be requested and the range of "events of default" that can warrant acceleration tend to be much more wide-ranging than those in a straightforward working capital facility. The scope for "technical default" or failure to satisfy all conditions precedent is therefore greater. The lender must appreciate that there might be risks involved in attempting to justify their actions — whether to accelerate a loan or to withhold drawdowns — on the strict wording of their documentation.

In the UK, as mentioned above, the principle of lender liability has not developed in the same way. The English courts are more likely to adopt a strict approach, based on the express wording of the contract between lender and borrower, and to resist arguments that seek to establish that obligations existed outside the terms of the contract as written. The issues of control and involvement in management could, however, arise in relation to English borrowers in the context of insolvency: potential liability can arise for wrongful trading as a "shadow director" or "connected person" and for fraudulent trading as a "knowing party". The consequences could include:

- the postponement of the debt and interest to the rights of other creditors;
- the making of an order for a contribution to the assets of the company; and
- the avoidance of previous payments and transfers, including floating charges, as preferences or as transactions at an undervalue.

Even under English law, there is scope for borrowers to allege that their banks have acted improperly and caused loss, for example, by misrepresenting the terms on which the loan financing would be made available. Third parties might argue that actions taken by the lender have induced the borrower to break its contractual obligations with them under, for example, negative pledge or borrowing restrictions in other loan agreements.

There are a number of ways in which lenders can try to minimise the risk that they will be called to account for their actions, whether under the principle of lender liability or analogous grounds as suggested in the checklist opposite.

Checklist: Avoiding lender liability

Suggestions for reducing the risk of lender liability include:

- ❐ covenants in the documentation should be drafted carefully to ensure that the lender is not seen to be effectively exercising control;
- ❐ restrictions might be better expressed as events of default, rather than as directions to follow specific policies;
- ❐ lenders should be careful when proposing to take an equity interest in the borrower and/or in having a nominee director on its board;
- ❐ lenders should take care to minute meetings with the project sponsors and borrower, to minimise the risk of allegations of misrepresentation or failure to negotiate in good faith;
- ❐ offers of finance should be clearly stated to be subject to final documentation and to be indicative, rather than exhaustive, of the terms and conditions of the offer;
- ❐ events of default should be specific (it is perhaps dangerous to rely solely on the ground of "material adverse change") and, where possible, subject to objective tests rather than simply being dependent on the discretion of the lender;
- ❐ financial covenants which could be regarded as imposing a "business plan" on the borrower should be avoided; it might be preferable for the lender to ask the borrower to produce its own business plan for approval and then to provide that failure to carry out that plan would be an event of default; and
- ❐ similarly, covenants prohibiting the borrower from removing existing management or board members might be better expressed in such a way that change of management constitutes an event of default.

Particular care should be exercised in a default, or rescheduling, situation, where the borrower is likely to be in a significantly weaker bargaining position than the lenders. If the lenders are going to take steps under their security to take over, in effect, the running of the project or to stop production and dispose of the assets, they should not ignore the possibility that the borrower or other parties involved in the project might allege that the lenders are liable on grounds of "lender liability" to compensate them for loss suffered as a result of their actions.

Chapter 5: Project documentation

(1) Underlying documents

Project lenders — and their lawyers — will need to pay careful attention not only to the drafting of their loan and security documents, but also to the documents of title and to the agreements entered into between the project sponsors and other interested parties which underlie the project itself and which might well be in place even before the lenders are asked to arrange the finance. The checklist overleaf indicates the range of documents that might be relevant.

In reviewing the underlying agreements, lenders should pay particular attention to:

- negative pledges affecting the project assets and cash flows on which the lenders rely for security and repayment; construction and sales contracts might well contain prohibitions on assignment;
- construction or operation contracts which require insurances to be effected by the contractor or operator with the result that the project sponsors are unable to provide the lenders with security or other direct interests in the insurances or proceeds;
- cross-default, negative pledge and "pari passu" clauses in other finance documents, preventing the creation of asset security in favour of the lenders;
- existing charges over the assets or revenues of the project or the project sponsors;
- set-off rights, which might, for instance, result in the borrower's failure to perform on other, unassociated, projects impairing the worth of the project being financed;
- pre-emption rights, consent requirements or rights of joint venturers to require pari passu security;
- loss or diminution of the borrower's rights on default under the underlying documents — by reason of, for example, failure to meet cash calls or to provide security for abandonment costs — or the exercise of other termination options;

Checklist: Project documents

Underlying project documents might include:

- ❐ concession agreements, government licences, royalty agreements;
- ❐ documents of title to land, including the obtaining of necessary surface and sub-sea rights;
- ❐ joint venture agreement between project sponsors;
- ❐ shareholders' agreement;
- ❐ constitutive documents of project company;
- ❐ project management agreement and technical consultancy contracts;
- ❐ construction contract and sub-contracts;
- ❐ contractors' and sub-contractors' performance bonds and advance payment guarantees;
- ❐ other guarantees, eg, of obligations under sales contracts;
- ❐ project insurances;
- ❐ supply contracts — whether on normal commercial terms or supply-or-pay or tolling agreements;
- ❐ sales contracts — again, whether on commercial terms or under off-take, take-or-pay or take-and-pay arrangements;
- ❐ throughput agreements;
- ❐ technology/operating licences;
- ❐ planning and environmental consents;
- ❐ utility supply agreements — electricity, gas, water;
- ❐ refining agreements (where additional refining is required to put the production into saleable condition), transportation contracts; and
- ❐ other financing documents of the project sponsors.

- "force majeure" provisions that exonerate one or more parties from performance of their obligations;
- confidentiality clauses restricting the dissemination of information relating to the project sponsors or the project itself;
- compulsory abandonment or "take-out" provisions agreed between the joint venturers requiring one of them to assume the liabilities of the others in the event that they wish to withdraw from the project; and
- expiry and revocation provisions of licences and any conditions attached, including any restrictions on transferability.

In these and other cases, the lenders might have to insist that the underlying documents are amended or that third parties agree to waive those provisions which impair the lenders' ability to ensure that they are adequately secured and to ensure that the project will not be abandoned except in accordance with the tests set out in the financing documents. The lenders might have to agree to take on the responsibilities of the borrower to the other sponsors in order to secure this level of cooperation. In some cases the lenders might just have to take the risk that these provisions are not activated to their detriment.

When negotiating the project documents, project sponsors should be aware of the problems that they might be creating for their prospective lenders and themselves. In many cases it will be easier, quicker and cheaper to deal with the issues at the outset, for example, by incorporating waivers and exclusions in the documentation, rather than asking for changes and concessions at a later stage.

(2) Finance documents

The financing documentation will encompass:

- the basic facility agreement setting out the credit terms, protective provisions and "boilerplate" as indicated in the checklist overleaf;
- the security documents, outlined below;
- trust or other coordination or intercreditor agreements between project lenders and holders of security interests;
- guarantees, comfort letters and other support documents, outlined below;
- fundraising documents: note issue, commercial paper, tender panels or other equity/debt arrangements will have to be documented if borrowing is not the sole, or first, source of finance; and
- ancillary financing documents: swaps, options, caps and collars; these might be entered into with only one, or possibly a selected group, of the project lenders or even with a third party.

Checklist: Facility agreement

The terms and conditions of the basic facility agreement will include:

- ❐ the amount and purpose of the finance;
- ❐ the interest rate and debt service/repayment profile;
- ❐ commissions and fees payable to the arrangers, the agent bank and the lending banks;
- ❐ conditions precedent to lending — legal opinions, board resolutions, copies of all project agreements, delivery of security documents, government approvals, waiver letters, experts' reports and financial statements;
- ❐ limitations on recourse to the borrower and/or other parties; dedicated applications of cash flows;
- ❐ protective clauses — tax gross-ups, increased costs indemnities, alternative interest rates, market disruption, supervening illegality, default interest, judgment currency and general indemnities;
- ❐ representations and warranties — as to corporate status and capacity, due execution of documents, accuracy of all project and financial information, validity of obligations and ownership of project assets;
- ❐ project covenants — standard of workmanship; compliance with licences, laws and regulations; construction development and operation in accordance with development plan and feasibility study; maintenance of insurances; payment of taxes;
- ❐ coverage ratios and other financial covenants;
- ❐ restrictive covenants — borrowing restrictions, negative pledge, pari passu, restrictions on dividends and disposals of assets;
- ❐ events of default; acceleration procedures; enforcement of security;
- ❐ project completion, "conversion" and abandonment tests;
- ❐ financial and project information, projections, reporting requirements and project supervision;

- ❐ mechanisms for withdrawal of monies from proceeds accounts, insurance accounts and other "escrowed" accounts;
- ❐ agency provisions, payment mechanisms, interbank coordination and sharing of receipts;
- ❐ assignment and transfer provisions; and
- ❐ dispute resolution — choice of law and forum, appointment of process agents.

(3) Security documents

The security aspects of project finance are dealt with in more detail in Chapter 6. In this section we will simply indicate some of the documents that might need to be entered into to create or record the required security interest:

- ❐ mortgages or fixed charges over land, buildings and other fixed assets;
- ❐ fixed and/or floating charges over moveable assets, book debts and production/work in progress;
- ❐ assignments of rights under underlying project documents, such as construction contracts, contractors' and suppliers' performance bonds, licences and joint venture agreements;
- ❐ assignments of project insurances and brokers' undertakings;
- ❐ assignments of sales contracts, take-or-pay, throughput or tolling agreements and of revenues or proceeds generated;
- ❐ escrow accounts to control and, when necessary, retain cash flows relating to the project;
- ❐ assignments of long-term supply contracts, including put-or-pay contracts and agreements for supplies of energy and raw materials;
- ❐ assignments of project management, technical assistance and consultancy agreements;
- ❐ pledge of shares of project company, including charge over dividend rights; and

- notices, consents, acknowledgements, endorsements, filings and registrations "perfecting" the security created under the various charges and assignments.

(4) Support documents

Again, the issue of third party support is dealt with in detail in Chapter 6, the following list being an indication of the possible documentary requirements:

- support by project sponsors: repayment guarantees, completion guarantees, working capital maintenance agreements, cash deficiency agreements, letters of undertaking and letters of "comfort";
- indirect support by project sponsors: take-or-pay, throughput and put-or-pay contracts, unconditional transportation contracts, supply maintenance agreements;
- contracts providing for proper management and operation of the project by one or more of the project sponsors;
- support by host government: licences, approvals, concessions, expropriation guarantees, exchange availability undertakings; and
- insurance cover: commercial insurance, export credit guarantees, multilateral agency guarantee arrangements.

(5) Experts' reports and legal opinions

Before committing finances to a project, lenders might insist on the production of satisfactory reports and opinions from:

- engineers, as to the technical feasibility of the project;
- environmental consultants, as to the likely environmental impact of the project and applicable legislation;
- insurance experts, as to the adequacy of project insurances;
- accountants, as to the financial position of the project sponsors and capitalisation of the project company;
- legal counsel in the host country and the "home" jurisdictions of any party giving security or support to the lenders as to all or most of the matters reflected in the checklist opposite.

Checklist: Legal opinion

A legal opinion should cover:

- ❒ the legal status, power and authority of the parties to perform their respective obligations under the project agreements or credit and security documents;
- ❒ the binding effect and enforceability of the documentation;
- ❒ the ownership of and good title to the project assets;
- ❒ the need to obtain and comply with licences, concessions and other regulatory measures;
- ❒ the existence of any exchange controls, withholding taxes or other duties eg, stamp duties;
- ❒ the enforceability of gross-up clauses, default interest provisions and other indemnities;
- ❒ the pari-passu status of the borrower's obligations and local rules giving preferred status to certain creditors;
- ❒ the likelihood of local courts awarding judgment in foreign currency;
- ❒ the validity of the choice of law and forum for dispute resolution and the enforceability of foreign judgments and arbitration awards; and
- ❒ the existence and extent of any immunities from suit or attachment of assets.

Chapter 6: Security and support

(1) Security and the legal system

It is common in project financing for the lenders to take security over the project assets so far as this is possible under the laws of the country where the assets are situated. Where security has been created under, say, an English law method — such as assignment or floating charge — any attempt to enforce that security in respect of assets outside England could give rise to difficult considerations relating to conflict of laws, although the lenders' approach is often to use both "belt and braces" by taking any security that might possibly be relevant.

For example, in North Sea oil project financing where the security consists of assets placed outside the territorial waters of the United Kingdom but within the Scottish section of the UK continental shelf area, it is normal to take English law fixed and floating security over the borrower's assets as well as a Scottish law floating charge and a Scottish "assignation in security" (which is, broadly speaking, equivalent to an assignment).

However there might be reasons why it is inappropriate or impossible to obtain such security. In such cases, the lenders will have to rely on negative pledges — that is, binding commitments on the part of the borrower not to create encumbrances over its assets in favour of any third party. For example, in several hotel project financings in China, no security over the hotel was taken because of the impossibility at the time of taking any effective security over such assets in China. In at least one later hotel project there, a mortgage was granted, although in favour of an onshore institution that had given a guarantee to foreign lenders, or as a trustee for foreign lenders.

A negative pledge is a contractual commitment that, unlike a security interest, does not confer rights to ownership, possession, control or sale of the borrower's assets, nor does it confer any priority on the claims of the lender in the event of a bankruptcy or liquidation. If the borrower were to create security in favour of a third party in contravention of the negative pledge, it is quite likely that the security would — in most jurisdictions — be regarded as valid. Whilst the borrower might be liable for having breached its contractual obligations, this will be little comfort for the lender if the project assets are being relied on as a major source of repayment. In cases where the third party knew, or should have known, of the existence of the negative pledge, the lender might be able to challenge the validity of any security created in breach of it, but this will depend very much on the circumstances of the case and on the rules of the relevant legal system.

Many projects are undertaken in countries whose laws and legal systems are unfamiliar to the lenders. By their very nature, some projects will require local lawyers to consider questions that have not arisen before in that jurisdiction — a project might well be the first of its kind or it might involve an innovative structure. In these cases, lenders cannot assume that security will be available in the same way that it is "at home", or at all.

The floating charge familiar to English lawyers, and which is available in a number of other common-law based jurisdictions, provides a very convenient means of taking a security interest in (and thus a right to control) all the existing project assets and those which might subsequently be acquired by the project company during the course of construction, development and operation. From the perspective of the project sponsors, the floating charge has the advantage over "fixed" securities of allowing the company to acquire, process and dispose of assets — raw material supplies, stock in trade, cash and other "moveables" — without having to enter into fresh security documentation for each acquisition or to obtain releases or consents for each disposal.

In those jurisdictions which do not recognise the concept of the floating charge — and there are many of them — the extent to which an equivalent result can be achieved by other means will require close analysis, and often considerable ingenuity. Not infrequently, the security package over the project assets in the host country will be governed by local law, whilst the security over assets that are offshore — such as sales proceeds — will be governed by the laws of another jurisdiction.

(2) The nature of security — fundamental questions

Lenders might find that the local legal system gives them rights and powers that fall short of expectations that are based on the concepts of their own systems. To an English lawyer, "security" implies the creation of rights that attach to the assets themselves, not merely claims enforceable against the owner of those assets. These rights give the security holder certain powers, most importantly:

- the ability to prevent disposal of the assets by the owner or the granting of interests to third parties; and

- the power to take possession of, to operate and/or to sell and realise assets ahead of other creditors and any liquidator.

It is important that lenders to a project should, at an early stage, carry out some analysis of the legal framework for creation of security in the host country and other jurisdictions that might be relevant. The availability, or otherwise, of effective security could have a significant effect on the structure of the financing and on the overall allocation of risks and recourse between the parties involved. The checklist opposite indicates some of the areas that ought to be investigated.

Checklist: Taking security

The lenders' lawyers should establish:

- ❒ which assets the borrower owns and which it merely has a right to use (eg, under a licence);
- ❒ whether security can be created over user rights as well as ownership rights;
- ❒ over what project assets a fixed security can be created;
- ❒ whether floating charges are possible;
- ❒ whether security can be created over assets not in existence at the time of creation of the charge;
- ❒ whether security over moveable assets can be created without physical transfer of those assets to the mortgagee or pledgee; what degree of control must the chargee exercise over the assets to constitute a fixed, as opposed to floating, charge;
- ❒ whether there are restrictions on foreigners taking security, especially over land;
- ❒ what creditors will, by law, be preferred over a secured creditor;
- ❒ whether third parties (including joint venturers under the terms of pre-emption or similar rights in underlying documents) or a liquidator can interfere with the grant of security or with its enforcement;
- ❒ whether, on a default, the lenders will be able to appoint a receiver over the assets; whether the banks will be responsible for the receiver's actions or whether the receiver can be appointed as agent for the borrower;
- ❒ whether, on enforcement, the lenders will be able to control the sale of the assets or must there be a court sale or public auction;
- ❒ whether the ability to enforce security over claims against third parties (eg, debts, receivables, shares, bonds, notes) depends on obtaining the third party's consent or, at least, ensuring that it is aware of the security;
- ❒ what formalities need to be complied with to perfect security — notarisations, registrations, filings and stamp duties; and
- ❒ whether the security can be held by an agent or trustee for a group of creditors whose members might change from time to time (eg, through transfer of their participation in the facility to another bank).

(3) The negative and positive functions of security in project finance

Experienced project lenders have learned to accept that security over the assets of, for example, a transport infrastructure or a petrochemical, power or oil and gas project is taken largely for "defensive" or even bank regulatory or other requirements, rather than because the realisable value of the security will have a significant impact on the level of risk that the bank is prepared to accept. Indeed, if the realisable value of the security is estimated to be sufficient to cover the outstanding loan, it could be argued that it is hardly a project loan in the true sense.

This is where project financing differs from other forms of asset financing, in that the value to third parties of project assets might well be minimal — unless they were taking over the running of the project. By contrast, an asset in the form of a building, ship or aeroplane will always have some residual value that a lender can realise by disposal to third parties, albeit at a "forced sale" price.

A pipeline under the sea is of no value to anyone in the event that there is no oil to put through it. The same is true of a tunnel which is unable to attract sufficient traffic flow or a petrochemical plant which cannot produce a product of satisfactory quality or with a sufficient level of efficiency. If the operator is unable to make the assets sufficiently productive to produce the necessary cash flow to prevent a loan going into default, it is hardly likely that a bank (or anyone else) will be able to do better. In many cases, project lenders will be more interested in assessing the operator's proven capability than in costing the assets, since it is the success of the operator, rather than the value of the assets, which will determine whether the loan will be repaid.

The examples outlined above illustrate project failures which result in the security being of little value. It is, of course, possible to contemplate circumstances in which security might be enforced even though the project is viable: for example, where the borrower has become insolvent for reasons unconnected with that project. In such cases, the existence of an effective security package could be of significant value to the lenders who might be able either to run the project themselves or to find a purchaser to take it on as a going concern.

(4) Valuable security and support

Other exceptions to the rather negative aspect of security portrayed in the preceding section include those set out below.

(a) Cash derived from long-term sales contracts

Clearly, where there is a long-term sales contract, the ability to take an assignment of the moneys payable under that contract is a valuable security right.

If the contract is effectively a form of guarantee, such as a take-or-pay or throughput agreement, then the security created by the assignment of rights under that contract will be a critical part of the structure of the financing.

However, if the long-term contract is not equivalent to a guarantee, and payments depend upon production continuing from the project, as with a take-and-pay agreement, then the assignment is less valuable security, because payments under the contract will cease if production ceases; this might well be precisely when the "security" is most needed.

The value attached to security over medium-term sales contracts entered into on a purely commercial basis, particularly if on a fixed price basis, will be greater in limited or volatile markets, where such contracts provide an assured outlet and source of revenue for the project.

(b) Insurances

Lenders will usually take an assignment of, or joint interest in, the insurances taken out over the project assets. In the event of destruction or damage to the project assets, this will result in a direct cash receipt by the lenders. The lenders will then have to decide whether to permit the insurance proceeds to be used to rebuild the damaged asset or whether to apply the insurance moneys towards the debt, in which event there is unlikely to be any further significant cash flow unless the borrower is itself capable of replacing the asset. The insurance for a ship or aircraft loan will frequently pay off the loan. The same is not necessarily true for a project.

The problem of insurance is more acute where the damage insured is relatively minor but sufficient to delay completion or to interrupt operation of the project. To protect against an inability to have debt serviced in the interim, lenders might consider requiring consequential loss policies (delay in start-up, business interruption or loss of profit policies) to be taken out.

Project operators will need to ensure that they do not allow cover to lapse or otherwise be jeopardised. Not only must premiums be kept up to date, but all relevant information about the project — and any developments that might affect the risks covered — should be provided. Standards of care, skills and good working practice should be maintained according to the insurers' requirements. Lenders should always bear in mind that changes in policy or practice during the course of a project that are not notified might provide the insurers with a pretext for disputing liability in the event that a call is made under the project insurances.

Lenders will usually insist that the policies contain a "loss payee and notice of cancellation clause" which will provide for the insurers to make payments under the insurances direct to an account of the lenders (or their agent) and to advise them of any changes to the insurances, and of cancellations or non-renewals. If an operator is responsible for insurances on behalf of a number of joint venturers, it is usual for notice of the assignment to be sent both to the insurers and to the operator, together with directions to make payment of the proceeds of any claims into the insurance account established for the lenders.

Lenders might be able to protect themselves to some extent against the possibility that the insurances have been prejudiced by the borrower's action — or inaction — by taking out "mortgagee's interest" insurance on project assets over which they have taken security.

In some countries, regulations might dictate that cover is effected through local insurance companies; if this is not satisfactory, project sponsors and lenders might find that it is possible to arrange for some or all of the risks to be covered through reinsurance offshore.

Lenders will often require an independent insurance adviser to consider these issues on their behalf. However, where such advisers are also permitted to be brokers, care must be taken to avoid any conflict of interest.

(c) Specific tangible assets

In many projects there will be some specific tangible assets which can be separated from the project and sold elsewhere on the open market or used by competitors. However, in the context of a large project financing, it is unlikely that the realisable value of such items would be of great significance in relation to the overall debt. The assets specifically charged will usually include the following:

❒ *the tangible assets used in the facilities*: oil production platforms, terminals and pipelines, mining equipment and machinery and, generally, all of the physical moveable assets — plant and machinery, vehicles — which are used in connection with the project;

❒ *the land, buildings and other fixtures of the project company*: foreign lenders might be unable to acquire interests in property, necessitating a security structure involving the participation of local institutions holding the security for the benefit of the syndicate through sharing arrangements;

❒ t*he licence or other operating permits*: such licences are usually not assignable or transferable without the host government's approval and, frequently, are required to be held by a "national" of the host country;

❒ *rights under contractors' performance bonds or completion guarantees*: these can be assigned to the banks by the project company;

❒ *technology and process licences*: the grantors will often resist strongly the lenders' desire to have an unfettered right to transfer these on an enforcement in order to be able to sell the business as a going concern; but the plant and machinery might be worth little without the operating technology;

❒ *the goods being produced by the project, the sales proceeds therefrom and the project's bank accounts*; and

❒ *other rights*: rights under the underlying project agreements — joint venture agreements, construction and supply contracts, operating agreements, transportation contracts — and under energy or other utility supply contracts relating to the operation of the project or the facilities.

(5) Sponsors' support — guarantees and quasi-guarantees

The key to the successful negotiation of a project finance is to achieve a balance of risk-sharing between the project sponsors and lenders that is acceptable to all parties.

Lenders might require undertakings from creditworthy shareholders or co-venturers to ensure that the project will at least reach the production stage or, if it does not, to ensure that the shareholders will satisfy the outstanding debt.

Alternatively — or additionally — lenders might wish to see shareholders' equity committed to the project ahead of, or at least together with, their loans.

The finance can often be structured in such a way that the project sponsors are, in effect, guaranteeing repayment of the loan throughout the period of the project even though the "guarantee" might be dressed up in a different type of instrument.

The borrower or the project sponsors might have specific tax or accounting aims that will affect what type of support they are prepared to give and, more commonly, that will affect how "watertight" — legally — the support is.

Some methods of providing support are outlined below.

(a) Completion guarantees

In most cases, the risk of the project not succeeding from a technological point of view will be greatest during the period up to the completion of the physical facilities and of the productive capacity, enabling a reasonable flow of production and receivables. This is particularly true of large-scale infrastructure or BOT projects, characterised by:

- ❐ long construction periods with longer time-lag to profitable operation;
- ❐ capitalisation of interest during construction phase; and
- ❐ high risk/high cost construction phase compared with lower risk/low unit cost in the operation phase.

Consequently lenders might be prepared to take the risk that a project will continue to be functional once production has started, but will often require the project sponsors to undertake to ensure that the project will indeed reach the stage when production, at an agreed rate and to an agreed standard, has commenced.

The simplest way to achieve this is to require one or more of the project sponsors, on a several or joint and several basis, to undertake to ensure that "completion" — as defined by the performance tests stipulated in the finance documents — is achieved by a certain date, ideally (from the lenders' point of view) with a clear undertaking to repay the loan if it is not.

The existence of a completion guarantee makes the negotiation of the completion tests more complicated and increases the likelihood of dispute at the relevant time as to whether the tests have — or have not — been satisfied, particularly where "completion" marks the conversion of the loan from a recourse to a non (or limited) recourse financing.

If the completion guarantee does not specifically provide for repayment of the money lent, the lenders' position is complicated by the need to prove damages — actual financial loss — arising from the failure to complete. This will involve showing, with the aid of a mass of technical and economic evidence, precisely how the project cash flow would have been sufficient to repay the loan if completion had taken place in accordance with the terms of the guarantee. This can be a difficult, lengthy and costly process, compared to pursuing a claim for payment of a specified amount under a straightforward repayment guarantee.

(b) Working capital maintenance/cash deficiency agreements

In many ways maintenance and deficiency payment agreements provide comfort similar to a completion guarantee, except that they might remain in place beyond the completion date.

In essence, such an agreement would provide that the shareholders or sponsors of the project company undertake with the lenders to ensure — by subscribing for shares or by providing loan capital (usually on a subordinated basis) — that the project company will always have sufficient funds to complete and operate the project or, alternatively, to satisfy certain specific financial ratios that might have been negotiated.

A claim for breach of an agreement of this nature would involve the lenders having to prove actual financial loss and the lenders would have an obligation to mitigate that loss. In order to prove loss it might also be necessary first to enforce security and exhaust any other remedies that the lenders might have against the borrower or other project sponsors.

(c) Letters of comfort

Lenders and project sponsors frequently agree that the finance documentation will include letters of "comfort", "support" or "understanding" from the ultimate shareholders of the project company or from other interested parties. Yet lenders and sponsors alike frequently misunderstand — or purport to misunderstand — the expectations of the other side as to the legal nature of the commitments expressed in such letters. Often they will comprise a statement of present intentions to maintain ownership of the sponsor's present interest in the project company and to ensure that appropriate managerial staff will be seconded to it. The letter might contain a statement to the effect that, historically, the parent has supported its subsidiaries in their financial difficulties.

Sometimes, such letters will contain more than just statements of present intentions, encompassing undertakings that the lenders intend to rely on in the event of problems arising.

If lenders are looking for more than "moral" commitment, they would be well advised to ensure that the sponsors understand this from the start. They must make this clear to their lawyers too: there is no such thing as a "standard" comfort letter. Conversely, if sponsors do not intend to provide a legal undertaking, they would be advised to ensure this is clearly stated at the outset; in some cases there might be a presumption that arrangements between commercial parties are intended to give rise to legally binding obligations.

(d) Take-or-pay and take-and-pay contracts

Take-or-pay and take-and-pay contracts can be defined as long-term contracts to make periodic payments, in certain minimum amounts, for the supply of services or goods.

The expressions are often used interchangeably and to mean different things in different contexts. In the case of a "true" take-or-pay contract, the crucial thing is that the obligation is unconditional; payment must be made whether or not the services are actually rendered or the goods actually delivered.

The expression "take-and-pay" is probably more commonly understood to mean a contract in which the obligation to make payment — or to accept the product — only arises if the product or service is actually tendered. References to take-or-pay and take-and-pay contracts in this chapter and elsewhere should be read as referring to arrangements which can be distinguished in this way.

Whether a take-or-pay contract can be obtained in relation to any particular project will depend on the nature of that project and the market in which it is operating.

Typically, the amount of the payments under a "true" take-or-pay contract has to be at least sufficient to service all — or an agreed part of — the obligations arising under the financing and the operating and other expenses of the project. It is fundamental that the underlying "hell or high water" obligation is watertight and that the contract is not cancellable.

The rights under this contract will usually be assigned to the lenders who will therefore have a direct claim under it against the party or parties who are obliged to take-or-pay.

If the level of production generates payments that exceed current debt service and operational requirements, the purchaser will still be required to pay, but the payments might be treated as being credited against sums due for future production in excess of debt service, rather than being released to the project sponsors.

The purchaser under a take-or-pay contract is likely to be one of the project sponsors and the project documentation will usually grant the purchaser some degree of protection against exposure to project failure. For example, the take-or-pay contract might provide for the purchaser to have the right to take over the project if the project company fails to maintain a satisfactory level of production.

The underlying project documentation between the project sponsors might well provide other protection for the purchaser, by ensuring continuity of supplies of raw materials to the project, ideally in amounts and at prices which can "match" the debt service and repayment profile of the financing and thus ensure that the purchaser will actually get what it has to pay for. The project documentation might also provide further comfort for the purchaser in the form of undertakings for the transportation of production.

(e) Throughput agreements

The concept of a throughput agreement is very similar to a take-or-pay contract and is, again, intended to be the equivalent in commercial terms of a financial guarantee. Its availability will be dependent on the type of project and the commercial environment in which it is being funded.

An early example of this type of financing was a petroleum project in the North Sea in which the participants were large oil companies who were the joint holders of the relevant licence.

The co-venturers formed two pipeline companies to construct and operate an oil pipeline from the oil field to England and also a gas pipeline from the field to

Germany. The oil companies then entered into a throughput agreement with the pipeline companies under which they agreed to pass sufficient oil and gas through the pipelines at agreed tariffs so that the cash earned would be sufficient to enable the pipeline companies to meet all of their financial obligations.

Once again there was a "hell or high water" provision, so that if, for any reason, it became impossible to pass oil or gas through a pipeline then cash payments would be made, equivalent to the amounts needed to enable the pipeline companies to meet their commitments. (Such payments might be characterised as "capacity reservation fees".) The pipeline companies assigned the benefit of this throughput agreement to their lenders so that the lenders had the right to receive the payments and to enforce the agreement against the oil companies, if they needed to.

(f) Tolling agreements

Like throughput agreements, "tolling" applies to projects which offer a service, such as smelters or refineries, where the tolling party's property is processed in some way by the project company and then returned to it. The tolling party will be required to supply materials for tolling such that the tolling fees will cover the project's debt service and operating costs "come hell or high water". Some power projects have also effectively been structured in this way with the utility providing sufficient fuel for conversion into power taken off by it and paying conversion fees which are adequate to provide this cover.

(g) Supply-or-pay agreements

Sometimes referred to as "put-or-pay" these arrangements focus on the supplier — of energy, raw materials or products — rather than the purchaser, and require the supplier either to provide the necessary input or to make payments in an amount sufficient to enable the project company to get the supplies from other sources.

(h) Forward purchase agreements and production payments

These arrangements are described in detail in Chapter 3 as alternative structures used in project financing where tax or accounting considerations dictate that a conventional "lender–borrower" structure should not be used.

These techniques usually involve the use of a quasi-guarantee arrangement similar to take-or-pay to ensure that the lenders' interest in the oil, gas, minerals or other product is turned into cash in the required amounts and at the required times.

To provide against there being insufficient production to pay off the financing, the seller or borrower might be required to make "deficiency payments" in lieu of delivery of production. These payments will in turn be sufficient to discharge the financing. Of course, if the lenders are prepared to take the risk of production reaching certain specified levels by a certain date, it might be the case that such deficiency payments can be dispensed with or, at least, reduced.

(6) Contractors' bonds

In construction projects, project sponsors and lending banks will be concerned to secure the performance of contractors, sub-contractors and suppliers by requiring bonding from banks or surety companies.

The bonds will usually constitute unconditional on-demand payment obligations in favour of the project company either in the form of a bond, guarantee or standby letter of credit.

Lenders will take assignments of the bonds to ensure that calls on them result in payments being made to accounts controlled by the lenders, and to ensure that — if need be — the lenders themselves can make demand for payment.

The types of bonds that might be required are:

- *bid (or tender) bonds*: whereby the bidders for a construction contract commit to take on the contract, if offered, on pain of forfeiting, say, 1% or 2% of the contract price;

- *performance bonds*: which effectively guarantee performance by the contractor for a certain proportion (perhaps 5% or 10%) of the contract price;

- *advance payment guarantees*: if the construction contract provides for the project company to make an advance payment to the contractors to assist them in buying the materials and equipment needed to start construction, the contractor might be required to provide a guarantee to refund the advance payment in the event of its failure to perform;

- *retention money guarantees*: the construction contract might provide for the project company to retain a specified percentage of one or more of the progress payments, in order to cover rectification of defects which might not be immediately apparent; the contractor can often ensure that no retention is made, by providing a guarantee in an equivalent amount; and

- *maintenance bonds*: these are bonds to cover defects which are discovered after completion of construction, within the "maintenance period" specified in the construction contract. In some cases, equivalent cover can be obtained by extending or renewing the existing performance bonds and retention money guarantees at completion.

(7) Host government support

In many projects, particularly those crucial to the infrastructure or national security of the host country — roads, railways, airports, hospitals, military bases — the host government will be closely involved in all stages of the planning, financing, construction and operation of the project. This is very much the case in BOT projects where the host government expects to take over the project after the initial operating phase.

In other projects, governmental support might be less direct, yet still crucial to the success of the project; projects for the extraction of natural resources and those which levy tolls on the travelling public will require licences or concessions. Other projects might depend on governmental support to ensure guaranteed supplies of energy and communications, to acquire land and develop the project site, to bring in foreign management and other personnel and to reach an understanding about environmental implications.

In each of the cases outlined above, the project sponsors and lenders will look to the host government to provide a positive contribution to the success of the project. The parties might also seek assurances that the host government will not take steps which will jeopardise the technical or economic feasibility of the project or the ability of the sponsors — and the lenders — to make the desired returns on their investment. This negative aspect of host government support involves a consideration of the "political risks" attaching to that country — the prospects of expropriation, nationalisation, restrictions on repatriation of dividends and profits and the other issues outlined in Chapter 4(5).

(8) Licences and concessions

In many cases, the right to establish, develop and operate a project will be founded on a licence or concession from the government of the country in which the project is to be situated.

The licence or concession will frequently be issued under regulations which give the host government widely stated rights to revoke it if certain events occur. Further, there is the risk to the lenders, where co-venturers are involved, that the licence will be capable of being revoked not merely through any act or omission of the borrower with which the particular lender is concerned but also through an act or omission of any other member of the consortium. There is also the risk that a default in relation to another, unrelated, development in the licence area might put the licence in jeopardy even though the particular project that the lenders are financing is running smoothly. Additionally, the licence might impose substantial obligations on the licensee which must be performed by set dates, under threat of forfeiture or revocation.

Lenders might look for comfort on a variety of issues, including:

- the host government's approval of the financing;
- the host government's approval of any plans for development and operation of the project;
- assurances that the government will not be seeking to impose direct or indirect restrictions on production or depletion which would have any material adverse effect on the projected cash flow;
- whether the lenders will be permitted to take a security interest in the licence or concession and, if so, whether that security will be enforceable without the need for further consents or approvals;

- the terms upon which any new licence will be granted in the event that the original licence is revoked;
- the ability of the lenders to have notice of and some right to be able to remedy breaches of the licence before the host government exercises its rights to revoke;
- the lenders' rights to take over and operate the project upon a default and to transfer the licence to a new operator;
- assurances regarding the tax treatment to be applicable to the project and the financing;
- assurances regarding the rate of royalties and other charges to be imposed by the government; and
- the intentions of the grantor with regard to any positive obligations imposed under the licence or concession: for example, in North Sea oil financings, the UK government has the right to require unitisation of oil fields (development of fields straddling two or more licence areas).

In this area lenders often have to be prepared to assume a degree of political risk. Project sponsors and lenders should remember that governments might be reluctant to restrict their own freedom of action, on grounds of national interest or sovereignty. Constitutionally it might be impossible for states or state entities to be as flexible as the sponsors or lenders would wish, even where there are perceived political or economic advantages in adopting a particular project structure. Governments will often resist committing themselves contractually to do more than have consultations to try to achieve mutually desirable ends.

Another issue arises when the development of only part of a concession is being funded. In these circumstances, lenders will need to consider how funds are to be raised by the licensee (and any other co-venturers) to enable it to complete the performance of obligations relating to the other part of the concession.

(9) Political risk insurance

Political risks can be insured against by project sponsors, suppliers and purchasers — as well as lenders — with private commercial agencies or with the assistance of governmental or multilateral agencies whose role is to promote exports, trade or development in the host country, sometimes in parallel to aid programmes or trade treaties.

The agencies providing this cover in the G-7 countries are:

Canada	Export Development Corporation (EDC);
France	Compagnie Française d'Assurance pour le Commerce Extérieur (COFACE);

Germany	Hermes Kreditversicherungs AG and Treuarbeit AG Wirtschaftsprüfungsgesellschaft (Hermes);
Italy	Sezione Speciale per l'Assicurazione del Credito all'Esportazione (SACE);
Japan	Export–Import Insurance Division of the International Trade Administration Bureau of the Ministry of International Trade and Industry (EID/MTI);
UK	The Export Credit Guarantee Department (ECGD); and
US	The Export–Import Bank (EXIM).

Whilst the support available differs from country to country, project sponsors, lenders and other interested parties can apply for some degree of protection against:

- war, insurrection or revolution;
- expropriation, nationalisation or requisition of assets; and
- non-conversion of currency and imposition of discriminatory exchange rates.

These agencies will often provide cover to guarantee exporters of essential supplies to the project and performance by contractors.

The World Bank (for public sector projects), International Finance Corporation (for private sector projects) and regional development banks, such as the European Investment Bank, the European Bank for Reconstruction and Development (EBRD) and the Asian Development Bank can be approached to support projects in developing countries and less-favoured regions. The World Bank's Multilateral Investment Guarantee Agency (MIGA) has recently extended membership to countries in Central and Eastern Europe, such as Hungary and Poland.

Chapter 7: Selected problem areas

This chapter highlights some of the issues that commonly upset the negotiations, and the negotiating parties, requiring them to reassess their basic understandings of the transaction or to pull out of the deal altogether.

(1) Basic understandings

Some of these "deal-breakers" arise because of misconceptions about the nature of project financing, as outlined in Chapter 1(7), namely:

- the level of commitment of equity and resources by the sponsors;
- the degree of recourse to the sponsors through "quasi-guarantee" arrangements;
- the real value and purpose of security over project assets; and
- the allocation of force majeure and political risks.

Other problems arise because it is often not possible to identify in advance the balance of the risk-sharing between lenders, sponsors, suppliers, purchasers, government agencies and other interested parties until the precise extent and nature of the risks is revealed in the process of negotiating the legal documentation.

(2) Conversion

"Conversion" is a term used to define the time when a project loan which started with shareholders' support, or with full recourse, becomes a loan with no shareholder support, for example, by the guarantee dropping away, or becomes limited recourse (ie, the claims of the lenders are limited — to some degree — to the project assets and cash flows).

The effect of losing shareholder support will usually mean an increase in the interest rate. The interest rate might, however, fall if the greater project risk during the construction phase was reflected by higher margins rather than by shareholder guarantees.

The questions of when conversion is allowed to take place and how much of the loan might be converted will be matters of considerable negotiation. Conversion does not necessarily occur on completion of the project; in some cases, it might, for example, depend on a satisfactory operating "track record" being established and/or on certain financial ratios being achieved.

Disputes in relation to conversion can arise over:

- *The physical completion test.* In the case of an oil project, the timing of a conversion into a non-recourse loan will usually be determined by a physical completion test demanding satisfaction of at least the following criteria:
  - the approval of the completed physical production facilities by a firm of independent consultants, ensuring that the facilities, as built, comply with the specifications in the design or development plan which formed the basis of the project appraisal;
  - the continuous operation of the project for a certain number of days at a certain percentage of the maximum production rate projected in the design or development plan, eg, operating for 90 days at 75% of maximum production; and
  - the production of a certain number of barrels of oil within a particular period or, where a purchase contract requires minimum amounts of supply, evidence that this supply obligation can be fulfilled.

  Power plants and petrochemical projects will require equivalent tests. Additionally, in the case of power plants, there might be a need to demonstrate an ability to react to changes in demand in accordance with design criteria (for example, base load versus load follow). In the case of petrochemical projects, tests relating to quality/purity and efficiency standards might also need to be satisfied. In both cases, fuel and feedstock specifications will need to be clearly defined.

  By contrast, completion of a hotel is often more easily defined, for example, completion might be more or less when the hotel opens for business or when the architect's certificate of completion is issued.

- *Valuation of how much of the loan can be non-recourse.* In oil or mining projects, lenders might be prepared to permit that percentage of the loan to go limited recourse which is equal to a corresponding fraction of the estimated net present value (NPV) of the production. It is, however, a complex calculation to determine the NPV.

  In principle, the NPV is an estimate of the proceeds of the sale of production to be generated over the life of the financing — or the project — less all anticipated operating and transportation costs, royalties and taxes and all other expenses, but not including the repayment of the loan. The resulting figure is discounted to determine the NPV and the lenders will permit a certain portion of that value to constitute the non-recourse element of the loan.

  In some more sophisticated non-recourse loans, the borrower will have an option to repeat this exercise at specified intervals in order to enable it either to put further parts of the loan onto a non-recourse basis or to extend the repayment schedule of the non-recourse loan.

When calculating the NPV, it will be necessary to make a considerable number of assumptions — each of which can be the source of much debate — such as:

- the amount of proven reserves — which is usually determined by the findings of independent consultants;
- the price of oil (or whatever else is being produced by the project);
- the rates of tax;
- the rates of royalties or other concession payments;
- the level of operating costs;
- the production profile; and
- the rate of inflation, exchange rates and other economic factors.

(3) The expert

Quite apart from the question of any dispute that might arise as to who the independent expert is to be, there is also the question of to whom the expert is responsible — who appoints him and who pays for his costs. Perhaps most significantly, there is the question of whether the parties will accept a position of being bound by any independent determination made by the expert, for example, relating to proven reserves.

Normally the lenders will wish to retain a residual right to impose their own assessment on matters related to such matters as the NPV of the project but it will of course be in the borrower's interest to ensure that, if the lenders and the borrower cannot agree, the expert's view should be adopted. The lenders might insist on the right to exercise a veto over the economic assumptions which the expert adopts as the basis for drawing up projections.

The frequency and detail of experts' reports can be a source of disagreement; borrowers resent the interference, delay and expense and the opportunities for lenders to seize on short-term problems as a pretext for hindering the project in the longer term.

Whoever appoints the expert, the other party will normally want the documentation to provide a right for them to challenge the expert's conclusions; lenders who challenge experts' reports might, in extreme circumstances, be given the right to be "bought out" of the financing by the borrower.

(4) Release of cash flow

It will frequently be the case that the cash flow generated from a project is — or at least is anticipated to be — significantly in excess of the operating and debt servicing requirements at any particular time.

The borrower will wish to ensure that the excess cash will be released to it or to shareholders or other group companies free from any right of the lenders to claw it back in the event of a later deficit arising.

The lenders, on the other hand, will hope to achieve a situation where the whole of the proceeds of production are ultimately available for paying off the debt so that any excess derived in the earlier years could be called upon to make up deficiencies in later years. Where the borrower is required not to distribute surpluses, there might be tough negotiations on the scope of its permitted powers to invest these monies. From the lenders' point of view, the effect that exercise of any such investment powers might have on their security interests will be important.

Negotiations on the question of surpluses can be resolved in a number of ways. The lenders might be successful in persuading the borrower that surpluses should be automatically applied towards prepayment of loan outstandings (ideally, from the lenders' point of view, from the "back end" of the repayment schedule); conversely, the borrower might succeed in retaining surpluses. A compromise might be for the borrower to retain the cash, but to be liable to refund surpluses to the lenders in the event of a default within, say, six months, as an exception to the general principle of limited recourse.

(5) Accelerated application of cash flow

In a limited recourse financing it will often be provided that, after payment of all operating expenses, a fixed percentage of the remaining proceeds of production derived in any particular period will be applied towards service of the debt. However, lenders will be concerned to see that in specific situations — for example, events of default, force majeure, imposition of new taxes — this "dedicated" percentage can be increased to 100%. Identifying and agreeing the situations in which this should occur is no easy task.

In certain types of project, it might also be the case that the lenders will wish to include requirements for repayments or prepayments of principal in addition to the agreed amortisation schedule if production is at a faster rate than planned. In this way they will guard against the risk of more rapid than expected depletion of the oil, gas, minerals or other reserves.

(6) Loss of limited recourse

In order to give more "teeth" to the covenants imposed on the borrower in a limited recourse financing, lenders often try to impose the condition that the limited recourse nature of the debt is lost in the event that breaches arise which are regarded as being within the borrower's control.

For example, if there were a breach which related to developing or operating the project in accordance with good commercial practice, there would be an argument for providing that the loan should be put on a full recourse basis. On the other hand, if the breach arose from an arbitrary revocation of the licence by a government, that would be a "political" risk which might fairly be said to have been assumed by the lenders and so would not give rise to withdrawal of the limited recourse protection.

The documentation might well provide that limited recourse will fall away if the borrower were to cause a diminution in the value of the project security by taking a particular course of action or by neglecting to take preventative steps.

The allocation of "force majeure" risks frequently proves to be a source of much debate in this context. So does the threat of loss of limited recourse as a result of failure to perform covenants which involve the borrower spending money; reliance on such covenants, the borrower might argue, is an attempt to achieve full recourse through the back door.

(7) Abandonment

Sponsors will not normally enter into a project unless they anticipate a significant return on the equity to be invested. Lenders, on the other hand, once they have lent against a project, will be concerned to see that it is completed and worked out so long as the eventual proceeds will exceed, by however small an amount, the additional costs incurred in obtaining that production.

Consequently, the lenders and the borrower might have a very different idea of when it is appropriate to abandon further investment in the project: the lenders will not want the borrower to abandon the project unless it is seen to have a negative net present value, whereas the borrower will want to be able to abandon if it regards the NPV as indicating an inadequate return on future investments of cash, manpower and management time and effort.

This comparatively simple situation can be made much more complicated where there are several partners involved in the project and where the operating agreements or joint venture agreements provide for automatic abandonment in certain situations, unless one or more parties wish to continue and agree to take over the interest of those that wish to abandon.

Lenders should bear in mind the potential for "lender liability" (outlined in Chapter 4(8)) — to the borrower and to third parties — that they might incur if they insist that projects continue to be operated in circumstances where the borrower or sponsors would prefer to abandon.

(8) Insurance

There is considerable room for argument as to what risks ought to be insured against and as to what is a reasonable level of cover to be taken out in connection with replacement values.

In the context of oil exploration, the insurances are comparatively well established and the borrower need normally only take out such insurance as complies with "good oil field practice" or in accordance with pre-agreed standard minimum criteria.

Borrowers might object to provisions in the documentation that require them to extend cover or take out further insurances in the future at the lenders' request. Lenders will be concerned to retain some ability to make such demands, particularly in such contexts as liability for environmental damage, where the law in many countries is developing rapidly.

In other areas there might be significant differences regarding the appropriate level of insurances and risks to be covered: one particular area that proved contentious in a major leasing project finance in the United Kingdom concerned the question of potential future liabilities being imposed on a strict liability basis on owners of equipment and the question of the owner's right to insist upon taking out insurances in the future which were not available at the time.

An acceptable compromise might be to appoint an independent insurance expert to judge what is appropriate and what is likely to be available in the future.

The domestic law of certain host countries might require insurance to be taken out with local insurers and/or in local currency. To mitigate the risks of the creditworthiness of the insurer and of foreign exchange availability, project lenders might wish either to negotiate permission for the insurances to be maintained offshore, or to insist on reinsurance offshore, with security over the reinsurance proceeds. Providing project lenders with access to offshore reinsurance can be both commercially and legally problematic.

(9) Intercreditor and security-sharing issues

Project sponsors and lenders should not underestimate the difficulties which can arise in dealing with intercreditor and security sharing issues and the time which might be needed to resolve them. Such issues can be particularly complex in financings which involve the provision of credit by more than one lender or syndicate of lenders.

Lenders might be reluctant to cede control of their own rights and remedies to fellow lenders. Thus one lender might insist on being entitled to require the enforcement of security even if other lenders do not wish to enforce, whilst those other lenders might not be prepared to permit a joint security package to be enforced against their wishes.

The proceeds of enforcement of security might be difficult to allocate if not all lenders are to share equally in all of the security — for instance where some but not all of the lenders are to receive the benefit of a host government guarantee.

Lenders might look for unanimity as regards satisfaction of conditions of loan disbursement or drawdown, to avoid an individual lender being compelled to continue disbursing against its wishes.

Different lenders might have different perspectives towards these and other related issues, according to whether the lender is a commercial bank or has other priorities, such as an export credit agency, a regional development bank or a multilateral agency.

Chapter 8: The future

(1) New challenges

In previous chapters, we have outlined some of the concerns common to all project financing: the problem of allocating risks, particularly political risks, between the various parties involved; the importance of a satisfactory legal environment in the host country; and the need to be adaptable when attempting to structure projects in jurisdictions whose political and social, as well as legal, cultures might differ significantly from those with which project sponsors or potential lenders are familiar.

The last decade has witnessed a series of major shifts in the way that the world goes about its business:

- the virtual collapse of sovereign lending to developing countries in the early 1980s;
- the success of Japan and the newly industrialised countries of South East Asia;
- the emergence of new political and economic regimes in much of Central and Eastern Europe, encouraging foreign investment and new trading patterns with the West;
- the moves towards a single market in Europe by 1992; and
- the growing realisation of the need to curb the negative environmental impact of industrial practices and processes and to protect against the consequences of global climate change,

each of which has had a dramatic effect on the perceptions of governments, multilateral organisations, businesses and banks as to how economic success can be promoted through the development of a country's — or a region's — earning capacity and infrastructure. There can be little doubt that the 1990s will see further changes that will present no less major challenges and opportunities.

In this concluding chapter, we look at some of the areas that many project finance experts consider to have great potential for the promotion of enterprise, development and increased economic activity through large-scale projects of the type that this book has described.

(2) Project finance in Central and Eastern Europe

In the aftermath of the political changes in Central and Eastern Europe since 1989, the new governments have been working hard to establish legal frameworks for the new order.

The West, sensing opportunities for the stimulation of its own manufacturing and service industries and the expansion of international trade has encouraged the process of change by offering aid, investment and know-how, and — through bilateral trade and taxation treaties and insurance guarantees — has sought to ease the apprehension of investors.

The establishment of an environment conducive to market-driven economies and large-scale investment entails enormous challenges:

❒ ownership of property and the means of production has to be redefined;

❒ forms of business enterprise have to be created — or revived;

❒ laws creating adequate and effective forms of security and protection of intellectual property must be put into place to encourage the injection of capital and new technologies;

❒ privatisation programmes must be implemented with due regard to considerations of sovereignty and the need to ensure the provision of essential services to citizens;

❒ the machinery of state control of supply, manufacture and distribution has to be dismantled;

❒ the new market economies that emerge have to be established with appropriate safeguards against abuse; and

❒ action needs to be taken to deal with some of the worst environmental problems in the industrialised world.

The countries that have attracted most interest — because of their large markets, natural resources, infrastructure and relatively highly-skilled labour forces — are Hungary, Czechoslovakia, Poland and the Soviet Union. In each of these countries, foreign investment is viewed as an important part of the privatisation process.

Of the four countries mentioned, Hungary is perhaps regarded as the most conducive to foreign investment: joint ventures have been permitted since 1972 and over 2,000 now operate there. In 1990, a State Property Agency was set up to supervise the country's privatisation programme; its projects include the sell-off of the national airline, Malev.

Czechoslovakia has also introduced new laws which encourage foreign investment; privatisation laws were brought into force in April 1991. Recent joint ventures concluded under the new laws include Volkswagen's agreement with Skoda, and engineering company Triplex Lloyd's joint venture with Motorlet, Czechoslovakia's leading aircraft engine maker.

Recent developments in Poland include the proposed liberalisation of foreign investment regulations to enable the repatriation of all after-tax profits and to abolish the need to obtain permits for establishing foreign-owned companies. Foreign investment is still going ahead under the current restrictions: in the country's largest privatisation to date, Unilever recently brought 80% of the Polish detergent maker Pollena Bydogoszoz.

Table 1: Aspects of foreign investment

Country	Extent of foreign participation	Forms of enterprise	Privatisation of state enterprises	Repatriation of profits	Protection against expropriation	Tax on profits and tax holidays
Soviet Union	In joint ventures, up to 99%; there must be a Soviet partner. Otherwise up to 100%	Joint ventures; acquisition of shares in limited liability and joint stock companies	Very limited	Limited to hard currency but subject to detailed regulations	Compensation payable	30% tax on profits on larger foreign participation; 2 yrs tax holiday from date of first profits
Hungary	Up to 100%	Joint ventures, limited liability companies, companies limited by shares (public), partnerships	Transformation law in place; recent guidelines restrict foreign ownership in energy and utilities	Permitted within hard currency resources of enterprise	Compensation payable; decision subject to judicial review	35% tax on profits up to 3 million forints; 40% on further profits; 5 yrs tax holiday for "activities of special importance"; substantial allowances in other sectors
Czechoslovakia	Up to 100%	Joint ventures, limited liability and joint stock companies, partnerships	Privatisation legislation in force 1 April 1991 preliminary steps taken to reform state enterprises	Permitted within hard currency resources of enterprise	Compensation payable	20% tax on profits below CSK200,000; 40% on further profits; 2 yrs tax holiday at discretion of authorities
Poland	Up to 100%, not less than 20% (this minimum will probably be abolished shortly)	Limited liability or joint stock companies; acquisition of interests in existing Polish companies	Privatisation law in place, foreign participation initially limited to 10% without special consents	Permitted for hard currency earnings and for up to 15% of domestic profits (likely to be extended to all profits after tax)	Compensation payment guarantee	40% tax on profits; 3 yrs tax holiday, up to 6 yrs in "preferred sectors" (may change to a "loss carry forward" system)

Joint ventures with foreign participation have been permitted in the Soviet Union since 1987; several hotel projects have already gone ahead. Examples of other projects funded on a project finance basis are:

- an Ecu136m aluminium foil joint venture project, involving supply-or-pay undertakings from Soviet aluminium producers and offshore escrow arrangements for the hard currency capital contributions of the joint venture parties and for foil sales proceeds;
- a DM140m project for production of butyl and halobutyl rubbers in the Tyumen region; and

- modernisation and expansion of a polyethylene plant, involving an off-take commitment by Union Carbide to purchase the product at a discount to world market prices.

There is massive potential for exploitation of the Siberian oil fields, which contain 80% of the Soviet Union's potential oil reserves and 90% of its coal and gas reserves. Apart from the inaccessibility of the region and its inhospitable climate, the economic infrastructure (transport, power stations, housing) has had to be built from scratch. In the petrochemicals industry there has been a vast scaling-back of expectations as a series of huge joint venture projects for Siberia have been cancelled or postponed. One which has survived is the Tobolsk project, in which Western interests will take a minority equity stake and the first phase of which alone is expected to cost $2bn.

A thumb-nail sketch of the environment for foreign investment in the four countries mentioned is set out in Table 1.

(3) A note on the role of the European Bank for Reconstruction and Development (EBRD)

The EBRD, which opened in London in April 1991, is likely to play an influential role in the financing of public and private sector projects in Central and Eastern Europe in coming years. Its initial capital of Ecu10bn is relatively modest, but the EBRD expects, in addition to committing its own funds (either as limited development equity or "seed money" for larger-scale projects), to be influential in providing information and technical support for Western investors and bankers interested in doing business in the region. Sixty percent of its budget is to be allocated to private sector projects, 40% to public sector infrastructure and environmental projects.

The EBRD's objective is "to foster the transition towards market-oriented economies and promote private and entrepreneurial initiative in Central and Eastern Europe" through:

- *provision of technical assistance and training*: tackling skill shortages in accounting, management, banking, distribution and services;

- *evolution of a business environment conducive to the growth of the private sector*: implementing structural and sectoral economic reforms, including demonopolisation, decentralisation and privatisation;

- *upgrading of public infrastructure*: to support the functioning of modern competitive market economies using financing structures that encourage private sector investment;

- *the establishment of an efficient banking system and capital markets*: mobilising savings for productive investment;

- *restructuring of state-owned industry and privatisation programmes*: working with governments and investment banks, participating in both equity and debt financing to attract other investors and enhance confidence;

- *encouragement of small and medium-sized enterprises*: paying particular attention to economic sectors where strong productivity gains can be achieved in a short time-frame; and
- *focusing on regional projects and the environment*: promoting trade and projects within Central and Eastern European countries and with the rest of Europe and developing expertise in environmental policy and practice.

(4) Asia — a different approach?

The industrialised countries of Asia have gone about the process of economic reform and restructuring in ways which make a fascinating contrast with the strictly market-oriented programmes advocated by the EBRD and others in the West for the emergent democracies of Central and Eastern Europe.

In some countries, notably Hong Kong, the principles of a market economy were practised in their most pure form.

In contrast, in a number of other countries, new and revitalised industries were given protection from import competition, export incentives and favourable tax treatment to improve their competitiveness. Declining industries were helped to diversify or phase out, and re-training programmes were developed for the work forces. Exchange rates were set to encourage exports and savings and, by and large, revaluations were agreed to only after the new industries had gained a foothold in overseas markets. Foreign know-how was largely imported through the retention of consultants, licensing arrangements and by replication of Western technologies; there was relatively little scope for foreigners to take an equity share in the new industries.

Between the two extremes, many countries in the region and, in particular, those whose economies are now moving ahead most impressively, have pursued policies that permit protectionist measures where these are seen to be in the national interests whilst at the same time allowing market forces to dictate in other areas. These countries have also been prepared to give incentives, including incentives for foreign investment, where this has been thought necessary in order to develop the economy. It is interesting to note, however, a general trend in the region towards market-driven solutions and an increasing interest in privatisation and private sector involvement in previously state owned monopolies.

Striking the balance between protectionism, market forces and incentives for foreign and private investment, has been, for the most part, a spectacular success and the potential for large-scale investment in projects in Asia is immense and growing.

The problems of unemployment, higher prices and increasing foreign debt that are emerging in parts of Central and Eastern Europe, as the structures of the old regimes are being dismantled, may cause reformers there to reflect on the different paths that can lead to a more successful economic future. Stanley Katz, a consultant to the EBRD and former vice-president of the Asian Development Bank, argues that:

> Common to both Asia's and Eastern Europe's economic restructuring efforts is the need to enlist and maintain public support for the reform process. Asia's NICs have demonstrated that it is possible to achieve market-driven economic restructuring without incurring unacceptably high economic and social costs. Eastern Europe's economic reformers might find it rewarding to take a closer look at Asia's experience. *(Financial Times, 24 April 1991)*

(5) Project finance in China

Joint ventures with foreign participation have been permitted in China since 1979 as part of the "open policy" to encourage foreign investment and trade, the injection of capital and transfer of Western technologies.

Foreign companies are now involved, either as investors, lenders or providers of know-how in such diverse areas as nuclear power and chewing gum, offshore oil development and hotel management. Whilst the regulatory system remains complex and multi-layered and the investment climate remains to some extent clouded by the events of June 1989, which led to the suspension of money market-oriented reforms, China continues to be perceived as having immense long-term potential for investment in large-scale project work.

The Seventh Five Year Plan, which was put into place in 1986, established as a priority the need to push forward vigorously the construction of "key projects" in the sectors of energy, raw and semi-finished materials, transport and communications. The Eighth Plan, taking effect in 1991, has confirmed this approach. To date, there has been relatively little in the way of limited recourse project financing but there are a number of reasons why such techniques might well be favoured in preference to conventional borrowing.

China's "open policy" has been conducted with caution: the rigid approval procedures and the debt registration system have kept her foreign debt down to around $40bn (June 1990), which is comparable to Poland's debt (prior to the recent write-offs). Much overseas borrowing has been contracted by non-governmental entities; the prohibition on government agencies giving guarantees to foreign loans reflects the policy of keeping out of the "debt trap" into which many other developing countries have fallen.

The limited recourse nature of project financing is attractive to the Chinese in the context of these policies, and lenders can achieve a commercial deal approximating the effect of guarantees by employing techniques such as the take-or-pay arrangements characteristic of project finance.

The earliest example of a concluded limited recourse financing in China is the HK$4.2bn Shajiao Coal-Fired Power Plant — "B" Station in Shenzhen, Guangdong Province. The project structure can be outlined as shown in Figure 1.

Figure 1: Shajiao — B coal-fired power plant: project structure

1. (See (a).) The project has been developed as a joint venture between the Chinese entity with responsibility for development of the power industry in the Shenzhen Special Economic Zone and a Hong Kong-incorporated SPV with Chinese, Hong Kong and Japanese shareholders.

2. Under the joint venture agreement, the SPV is responsible for concluding construction, supply and off-take contracts and for raising the foreign currency finance. Following completion, the SPV will operate the plant for 10 years — assuming responsibility for meeting all project expenses and debt service and retaining net revenues. At the end of the period the plant is transferred to the Chinese party without compensation: in effect, a BOT structure.

(a) The joint venture

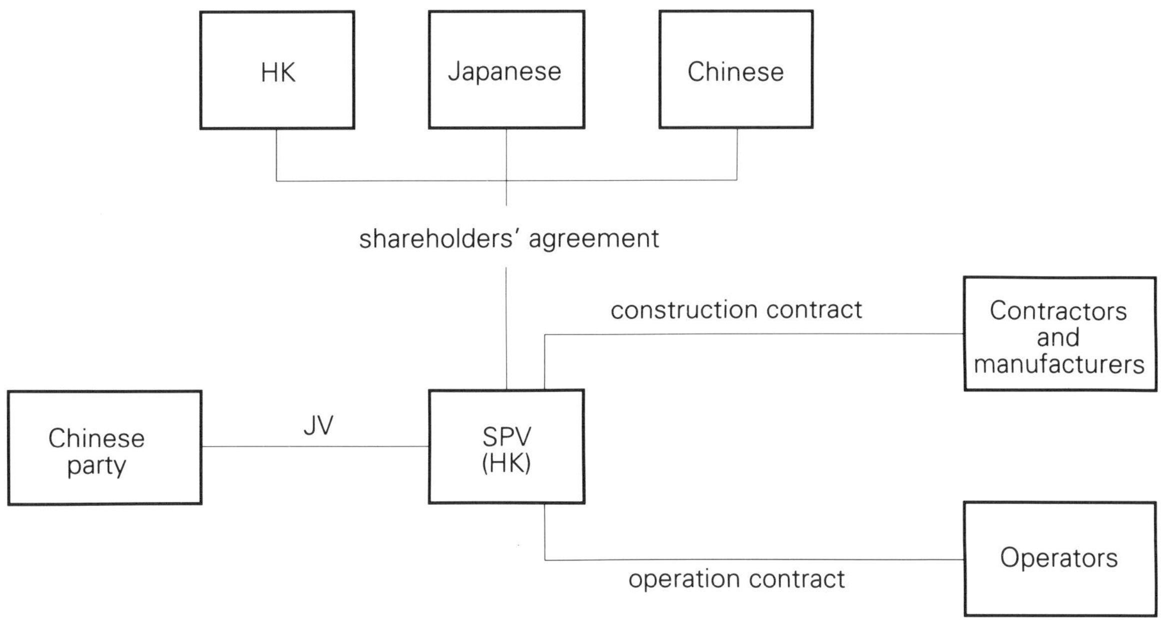

(b) The finance

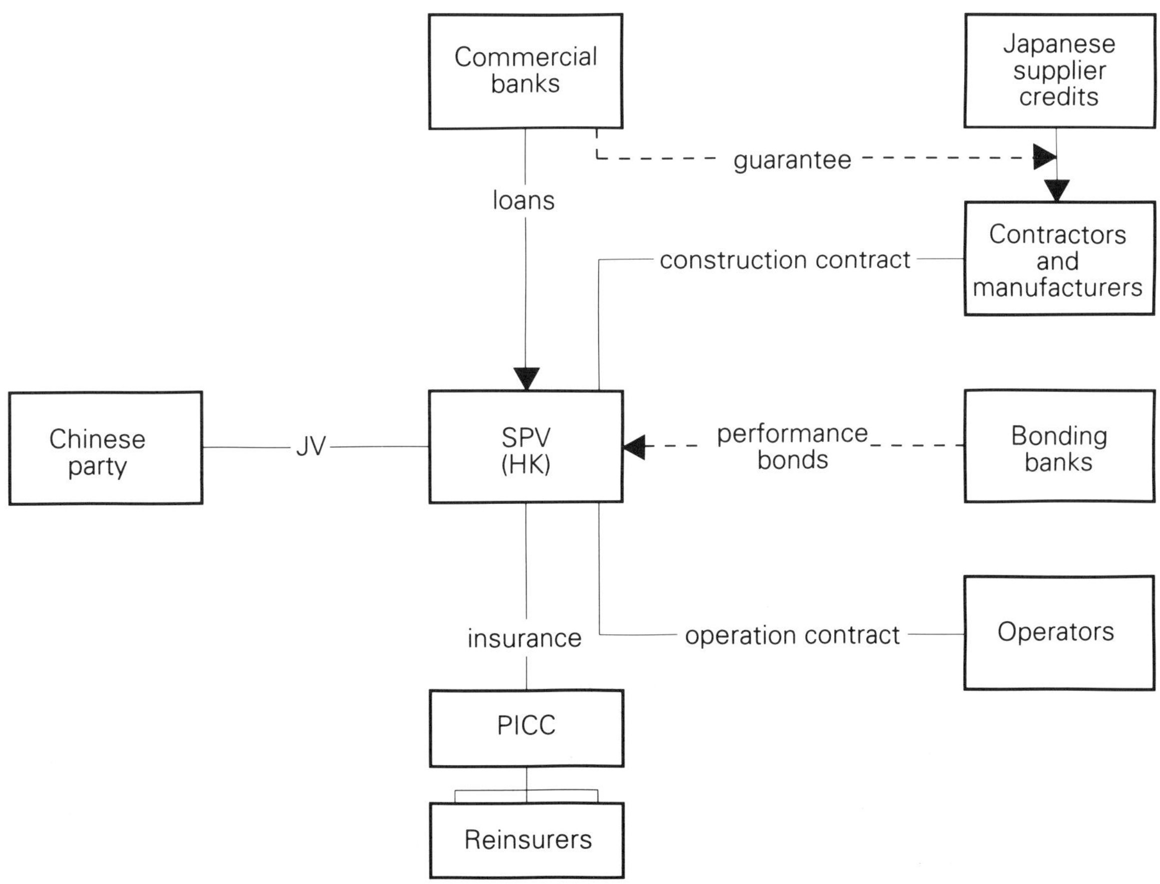

3. (See (b).) Construction and manufacture of equipment is undertaken by a consortium of Japanese and Hong Kong companies on a turnkey contract basis. They are financed by Japanese supplier credits, with the deferred element of progress payments under the contract being guaranteed by a syndicate of commercial banks. (Note: the supplier credits have since been refinanced to achieve cheaper fixed-rate funding; the syndicate's guarantees have been replaced by loans used to prepay the contractor.)

4. Further finance is provided by way of loans from the syndicate to the SPV.

5. Operation of the project is undertaken, for an initial period, by a consortium of internationally reputable power station operators (one of whose tasks is to train local operators); insurance against physical damage and consequential loss is provided through the People's Insurance Company of China (PICC).

(c) Off-take, guarantees and comfort letters

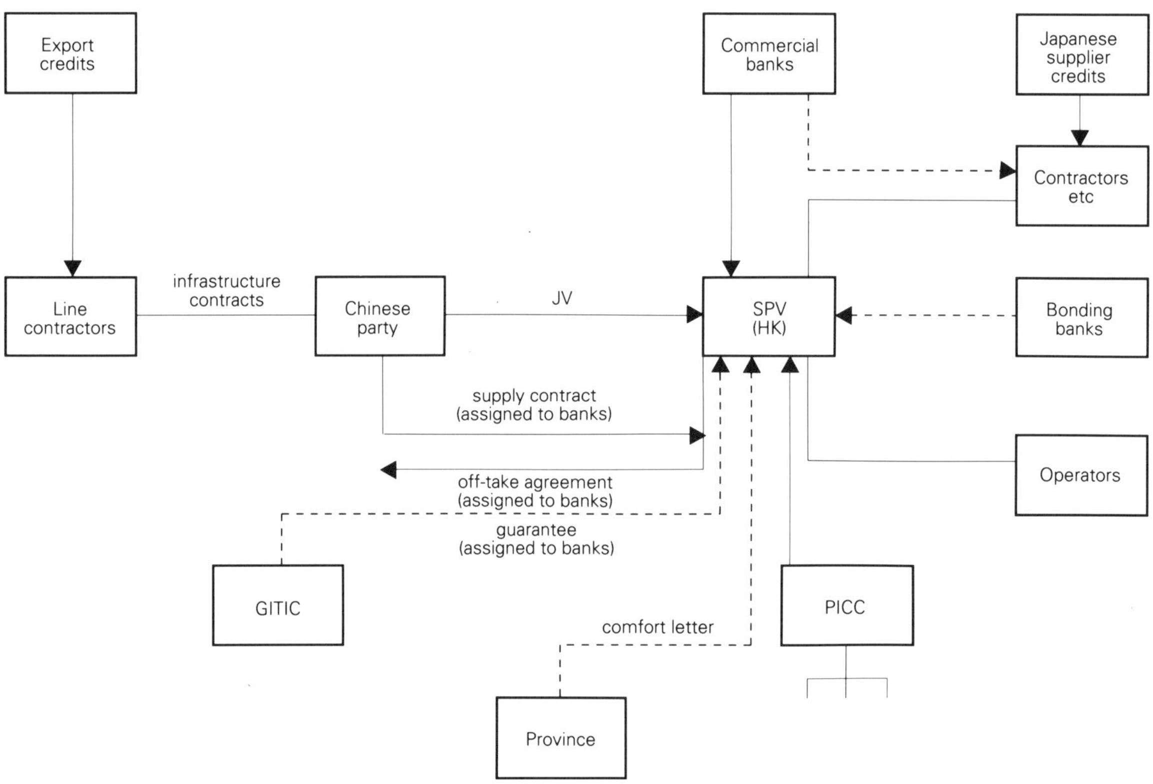

6. (See (c).) The Chinese party supplies coal to the plant at a fixed price and, under an off-take agreement, takes a minimum amount of power production at agreed prices, sufficient to meet projected expenses, debt service and expected return on the sponsors' investment.

7. The Chinese party's obligations are guaranteed by an "Authorised Guarantor", the Guangdong International Trust and Investment Corporation (GITIC). The guarantee is assigned to the commercial banks. A comfort letter is provided on behalf of the Provincial government.

8. The Chinese party is responsible for putting in place the transmissions line infrastructure (financed largely through export credits on a non-project risk basis).

The Chinese legal system has developed considerably since the financing documentation was signed in 1986, but many of the issues that had to be resolved in the documentation for Shajiao — B are still not specifically addressed in the legal and regulatory framework. Accordingly, the documentation surrounding this transaction is likely to continue to be of substantial reference value for some time to come.

(6) Legal frameworks in South East Asia

Whilst enthusiasm for taking on large-scale projects in China might have declined somewhat in recent years, a more positive mood surrounds the prospects of doing this type of business elsewhere in South East Asia, in particular in Thailand, Indonesia and Malaysia; one major project has been concluded recently in the Philippines and proposals are beginning to emerge in relation to Vietnam.

The rapidly developing economies in these countries are dependent on the development of infrastructure, be it in the form of transport and communications, energy or heavy industry and petrochemicals. They also have substantial natural resource reserves within their boundaries which they wish to develop. The availability of low cost labour and investment incentives has made them attractive manufacturing bases for foreign investors. Their potential as tourist destinations has also generated interest.

These factors have given rise to substantial project activity in the region. Projects such as toll-road and mass transit systems, power stations, steel plants, mining and oil and gas production, refinery and downstream plants and hotel and resort facilities have all been successfully financed in recent years. Many more are proposed, a number on a build-operate-transfer (BOT) basis.

Some of the features of the legal framework for doing business in these countries are outlined below.

(a) Thailand

(i) Foreign ownership

Foreign ownership of local companies is governed by the Alien Business Law. For certain businesses, (for example, banking, commercial transportation, ownership of land and certain areas of local manufacturing) a company must be owned at least as to 51% by local shareholders, unless investment promotion privileges have been granted by the Board of Investment (BOI). Whilst other types of business are generally open to majority foreign-owned companies, permits will only be granted if that business could not be competently carried on by a majority Thai-owned company.

(ii) Incentives for foreign investors
The BOI is responsible for promoting foreign and domestic investment; it might grant tax incentives, investment protection guarantees and tariff barriers to attract investors. Special consideration will be given to export-oriented projects, those forming the basis for further industrial development and those which create substantial employment. Additional incentives are available to companies located in Investment Promotion Zones.

(iii) Exchange controls
Exchange controls are administered by the Bank of Thailand under the Exchange Control Act. Although there are no restrictions on foreign borrowings, all foreign borrowings by Thai residents must be converted into Baht through an authorised agent of the Bank of Thailand within a specified time following receipt or deposited without conversion into a foreign currency account with an authorised agent. An authorised agent of the Bank of Thailand must approve the purchase of foreign currency to service foreign currency obligations.

(iv) Withholding tax
Withholding tax applies to interest, dividends and other assessable income payable to non-residents. The rate is 25%, which is reduced to 10% in the case of interest payable to a bank or financial institution. Reductions might be available through the numerous double tax treaties: Thailand has concluded at least 25, including treaties with France, Germany, Japan and the UK.

(v) Security
Security can be created in various forms, including by way of registered mortgages over immoveables (eg, land) and certain moveables, including ships and machinery registered under the Machinery Registration Act. Thai law does not, however, provide for mortgages over aircraft. Pledges can be created over certain moveables (eg, shares, raw materials, stock-in-trade, securities and cash). Assignments can also be effected if the claim is regarded under Thai law as being assignable. However, Thai law does not recognise the concept of a floating charge.

(vi) Foreign law and judgments
A choice of foreign governing law will be generally upheld, except in relation to security over property situated in Thailand. Foreign judgments are not enforceable in Thailand, but might be introduced as evidence in proceedings before a Thai court.

(b) Malaysia

(i) Forms of business enterprise
The most common forms of business entity are the limited liability company and the partnership (which cannot have limited liability). Both are affected by the government's National Development Policy which regulates foreign investment. The guidelines set out in the Policy should, in practice, be followed even though they do not have the force of law.

(ii) Foreign ownership

Whilst 100% foreign ownership might be allowed in some export-oriented and labour intensive activities, foreign ownership will usually be restricted; in some areas (such as, mining) no foreign ownership will be permitted. Where restrictions apply, they generally seek to ensure that foreign ownership is limited to 30% and control remains with the local investors. However, any acquisitions by foreign entities which lead to a holding of 15% or more by a single entity or 30% or more in aggregate of a Malaysian company will require approval of the Foreign Investment Committee (FIC). FIC approval will also be needed to acquire assets in excess of M$5m. There are no foreign ownership restrictions for real property.

(iii) Incentives for foreign investors

Financial incentives, including tax breaks, are offered to foreign investors, mainly in the area of pioneer status manufacturing projects and export-oriented businesses.

(iv) Exchange controls

Foreign exchange restrictions require Bank Negara Malaysia (BNM) approval and consent to offshore loans in Malaysian Ringgit and offshore loans in foreign currencies in excess of the equivalent of M$1m. Special procedures and BNM approvals are required for remittances outside Malaysia in excess of M$10,000 (or its equivalent in foreign currencies). Guarantees in respect of offshore liabilities require BNM consent (prior to execution) to permit performance of the foreign currency obligations when the guarantee is enforced.

(v) Withholding tax

There is withholding tax at the rate of 20% on interest and payments in the nature of interest. Double tax treaties can effectively reduce this rate, for example to 10% under the double tax treaty between Singapore and Malaysia.

(vi) Security

Forms of security comparable to those available under English law are possible, with similar registration requirements. Powers of attorney (as security) must be registered in the High Court. Particulars should also be lodged at the Companies Registry. It is not uncommon to appoint a local security agent to facilitate enforcement and, in relation to more complex transactions, a security trustee arrangement is sometimes used.

(vii) Foreign law and judgments

The courts will generally recognise the choice of an external law as the governing law of a document except when it is contrary to Malaysian law or to public policy. Foreign judgments might be enforced subject to reciprocity considerations and registration in the High Court. There are no restrictions on awarding judgments in foreign currencies.

(c) Indonesia

(i) Forms of business enterprise

The most common form of business entity is the limited liability company, although there are a number of other forms which are also loosely categorised as "companies".

(ii) Incentives for foreign investors

Indonesia currently encourages private investment either in the form of domestic investment or foreign direct investment. The Investment Coordinating Board (Baden Koordinase Penenaman Modal, BKPM) is responsible for foreign investment application and formulation of the policy on investment. All foreign investment must be in the form of a joint venture with an Indonesian partner. The general rule is that, initially at least, 20% of the foreign investment joint venture company (or PMA) must be owned by the local partner and the local ownership must be raised to not less than 51% within 15 years after formation. PMAs are granted certain tax and accounting benefits, including exemption/relief from import duty on the importation of capital goods (such as machinery, equipment and spare parts) and advantageous depreciation and taxation rates.

(iii) Exchange controls

There are no foreign exchange restrictions as such. However, by virtue of a Presidential Decree, reporting requirements are imposed in relation to foreign currency liabilities. These requirements vary, depending on whether the obligor is wholly or partly state owned, or a foreign investment company.

(iv) Withholding tax

There is a withholding tax, at the rate of 20%, which applies to interest, payments in the nature of interest, fees and guarantee commissions made out of Indonesia. However, double tax treaties, such as that with Japan, can reduce the rate (in that case, to 10%).

(v) Security

The most usual forms of security are the hypothec (or mortgage) over land, fiduciary transfer of proprietary rights in stock, inventory and other moveable assets, deed of assignment of receivables and other intangible assets, a personal or corporate guarantee, the power of attorney to establish hypothecs, the power of attorney to sell land and the pledge. Formalities of language, execution and registration might need to be complied with.

Rights granted by virtue of any of the forms of security might be enforced by the party taking the security, although, as in the case of Malaysia, it is not uncommon to appoint a local security agent or to use a security trustee arrangement.

(vi) Foreign law and judgments

The courts will generally recognise the choice of an external law except where it is considered to offend fundamental concepts of public order. Some (but not all) Indonesian counsel also advise that, in order for a choice of foreign law to be upheld, there must be some connection with the country concerned. Security documents dealing with assets in Indonesia, must be governed by local law.

There is no recognition of foreign judgments, although a foreign judgment might possibly be of assistance in evidence. There are no restrictions on awarding judgments in foreign currencies.

(d) Vietnam

(i) Foreign ownership and investment

The Law on Foreign Investment of 1987 (as amended and implemented subsequently in 1990 and 1991) provides for three forms of permitted foreign investment, namely: a contractual business cooperation, a joint venture company and 100% foreign-owned company. Each must first be approved by the State Committee for Cooperation and Investment (SCCI). Foreign investment is possible in every sector of the economy.

The government has recently approved the Saigon Export Processing Zone, or Sepzone, near Ho Chi Minh City. It is proposed that Sepzone, which is to accommodate non-polluting industry of a light assembly nature, will be accorded a one-stop approval status which will enable export industries established there to receive immediate promotional privileges, such as reduced remittance costs and lower income tax.

(ii) Exchange controls

There is a strict system of exchange control, administered by State Bank of Vietnam (SBV) and applicable to all local and foreign companies. All foreign exchange must be sold to an authorised bank in Vietnam, which is then required to consolidate its foreign funds with SBV. SBV then reallocates foreign exchange back to the banks on a case-by-case basis for approved transactions. Foreign exchange rates are set generally by SBV every 48 hours. Businesses might hold overseas bank accounts if they have SBV approval, although in practice this approval appears rarely to be given.

Profits can be repatriated, although profits from export-oriented ventures have preference over import substitution schemes. Margin rules for letters of credit exist and are strictly enforced. For example, for sight L/Cs for import, the applicant must deposit the full face value of the L/C in the relevant currency with the issuing bank prior to issue.

(iii) Withholding tax

A withholding tax, normally of 10%, applies to payments of interest, dividends and other income to non-residents; this can be reduced to 7% or 5% in respect of repatriated profits, depending upon the size of the investment or the percentage ownership of the non-resident.

No double tax treaties currently exist, although drafts are being discussed with Australia, France and Italy.

(iv) Security

The local law on security is underdeveloped. For example the current lack of any proper concept of title means that real property cannot be considered as security. Financiers therefore invariably look to security offshore to secure loans made to a Vietnamese entity, for example, a charge over an offshore bank account (although this might not be possible if the necessary approvals of SBV are not obtained).

(v) Foreign law and judgments

The extent to which a choice of foreign law will be recognised is unclear. It is thought that it might be possible to adopt a foreign governing law if the particular contract does not fall within the Economic Contract Ordinance, for example, a joint venture agreement with a local entity.

(e) Philippines

(i) Foreign ownership

Foreign ownership of Philippine enterprises is generally limited to 40%. Certain businesses (for example, retail trade and small-scale utilisation of natural resources) are closed to foreign investors, but 100% foreign ownership (subject usually to a condition of eventual divestment over a relatively long period) is permitted in pioneer, certain export-oriented and Export Processing Zone enterprises. Foreign equity investments which are above the relevant threshold percentage will require the prior approval of the Board of Investments (BOI) but this requirement will be modified under new legislation referred to below. All foreign investments have to be registered with the Central Bank (CB) primarily for capital repatriation and profit remittance purposes.

In June 1991, the Foreign Investments Act of 1991 was passed to modify the rules relating to foreign ownership of Philippine enterprises. The 1991 Act provides for the introduction of a Foreign Investments Negative List which sets out certain investment areas in which foreign ownership is limited to 40%. Foreign investment up to 100% will be permitted, without the need for BOI prior approval, in enterprises that are not listed and which are categorised as "export" or (provided existing laws do not limit foreign ownership in such enterprises) "domestic market" enterprises. The 1991 Act is expected to be implemented in the latter part of 1991 pursuant to the announcement of relevant rules and regulations.

The National Economic and Development Authority (NEDA) is required by the 1991 Act to formulate and publish, within 18 months of the 1991 Act coming into effect, a list of industries strategic to the development of the economy and to specify, as a matter of policy but not as a legal requirement, the desired equity participation by the government and/or local investors in such industries.

(ii) Incentives for foreign investors

Enterprises with "preferred" activities listed in the Investment Priorities Plan or which are located in an Export Processing Zone can enjoy certain investment incentives. For example, an enterprise accorded pioneer status can enjoy income tax holidays of up to six years, income tax deductions of 50% of the amount paid as wages to direct labour, tax and duty exemptions on imported capital equipment and spare parts and employment of foreign nationals.

(iii) Debt for equity

In 1986, the government introduced a debt/equity swap programme whereby the CB will redeem (at the face value in Pesos) any Philippine debt instrument denominated in a foreign currency which an investor has brought in the secondary market provided that the investor invests such proceeds in certain CB-approved business activities. Guidelines have been revised recently with a view to providing additional incentives for investment in certain designated sectors of the economy. In July 1990, the government enacted a law (known as the BOT Law) which sets out the guidelines for the development of infrastructure projects by private investors.

(iv) Exchange controls

A strict system of exchange control is administered by the CB. As a general rule, foreign borrowing is allowed only to cover the foreign exchange cost of priority projects (for example, power/energy and export-oriented) embodied in the national socio-economic plan. Foreign currency proceeds must be converted into Pesos with authorised agent banks of the CB but certain receipts might be deposited, without conversion, with such banks.

(v) Withholding tax

Withholding tax applies to interest, dividends, and other fixed and determinable income payments to non-residents. Reductions are, however, available through double tax treaties, for example, with the UK, US and Japan.

(vi) Security

Security can be created in various forms, including mortgages over land and moveables and pledges over shares. Security documents normally have to be notarised and, in some cases (for example, relating to land), registered with the relevant registry.

(vii) Foreign law and judgments

A choice of foreign law as governing law is generally respected if the chosen law has a reasonable connection with the transaction.

(7) Other prospects

The opportunities — and challenges — facing potential project sponsors and lenders in various parts of the world outlined in this chapter are by no means exhaustive.

Long-term prospects, understandably viewed with great caution, exist for reconstruction and development in areas of the Middle East, devastated by conflict in recent years. The mobilisation of the funds of Islamic investors might play a significant part in this process.

In the middle-income countries of Latin America, struggling to overcome massive debt burdens, opportunities are emerging for investment through debt-equity swaps encouraged by the Brady Plan and other initiatives of the international creditor community.

In these and many other countries, there is a recognition of the need to develop or modernise the industrial base, to acquire new and cleaner technologies and to build an infrastructure capable of delivering energy, services and mobility to the business community and to society at large. Meeting these needs will involve the development of large-scale projects; in many cases, the task might be beyond the means and capability of the host country: capital, technologies and skills will have to be attracted from outside.

As the previous chapters have demonstrated, the existence of minerals or oil or potential markets might not of itself attract sponsors and lenders. The development of a legal and regulatory framework that is conducive to investment, and that offers some degree of security in the event of project failure or political or economic changes, is an essential element in building confidence in the potential for taking on such challenges. Sponsors and lenders can waste a lot of time, energy and money if they do not address at an early stage the implications of doing business in an unfamiliar legal environment.

This book has also attempted to show that successful project financing depends on the ability of each of the parties to appreciate the interests, concerns and limitations of the others and to adopt a flexible approach to structures to ensure that a bargain is struck that is acceptable to all, in terms of risk, responsibility and reward.

Appendix

Selected glossary of technical and banking terms

Amortisation — reduction of loan outstandings, usually in accordance with an agreed repayment schedule

Advance payment guarantee — a guarantee given on behalf of a contractor, for example, under a construction contract, for repayment of advance payments made by the employer in the event of non-performance by the contractor

Assignment — the transfer of title to an asset — particularly of contractual rights, claims and debts — absolutely or for purposes of security

Bareboat charterparty — a long-term contract for employment and use of a vessel

Bid bond — a bond given on behalf of a party bidding for a contract to ensure that it will enter into and perform the contract if its bid is accepted

BOT (build-operate-transfer) — a structure of project finance whereby the project company will build and operate the project for a period determined to be sufficient to discharge construction costs and generate a satisfactory return during the operating period, at the end of which the project is handed over to the host government, usually without compensation

Buyer credit — a financing arrangement under which a bank in the supplier's country lends to the buyer — or a bank in the buyer's country — to enable the buyer to make payments due to the supplier under a contract for supply of goods and/or services

Caps, collars, floors — techniques employed in hedging arrangements to minimise the effects of fluctuations in interest rates

Cash deficiency agreement — an undertaking, usually given by a parent company, to creditors of its subsidiary to ensure that the subsidiary will have sufficient cash to meet its commitments

Completion — satisfaction of the agreed tests for practical completion of a project, usually marking the end of the construction phase and the beginning of the operating phase

Completion guarantee — a guarantee, usually given by a parent company or sponsor, of performance of the project company's obligations to bring the project to the point of completion

Concession agreement — an agreement made between a host government and the project company or sponsors to permit the construction, development and operation of a project and, usually, to have access to public utilities

Conditions precedent — documentary and other conditions required to be satisfied before the borrower can request drawdown or other credit facilities to be made available under the terms of a facility agreement

Covenant — an agreement by a party to perform — or refrain from performing — certain acts, breach of which might constitute an event of default

Cross-default — an event of default triggered by a default in the payment of — or by the actual or potential acceleration of the repayment of — other indebtedness of the borrower or another company (whether associated or not)

Debt/equity swap — a transaction whereby the owner of a foreign currency debt instrument — usually for developing country debt — exchanges it for local currency-denominated debt securities or an equity interest in an enterprise in that country

Debt service	the payment of scheduled interest, fees, commissions and principal instalments under a loan agreement
Default interest	interest payable under the terms of a loan agreement on overdue amounts, usually at an enhanced rate
Depreciation	the reduction in the value of assets over time
Double tax treaty	an agreement between two countries to avoid or limit the double taxation of income and gains, whereby an investor resident in one country may apply for reduction of or exemptions from taxes imposed on his business by the other and/or be entitled to relief in respect of such income or gains in the investor's own country
Drawdown	a borrowing made under the terms of a loan facility
EBRD	the European Bank for Reconstruction and Development
EIB	the European Investment Bank
Equity	a company's paid-up share capital and other shareholders' funds, possibly including long-term subordinated loans
Escrow accounts	accounts into which a borrower or other party may be required to direct payment of receivables or other cash, and to which conditions apply restricting access to the funds; possibly charged in favour of the lenders
Event of default	an event which under the terms of a loan agreement entitles the lender to cancel the loan facility, accelerate payment of outstandings and enforce security (such as breach of covenant, insolvency, material adverse change)
Expropriation	the dispossession of assets by the state or a state entity, for example, under a nationalisation programme

Export credits credit or guarantee facilities made available to exporters to promote the manufacture of goods or provision of services for export

Feedstock the supply of raw materials, for example, crude oil, to a processing or refining plant

Finance lease a financing device whereby possession of an asset is acquired for use for most of its useful life; rentals over the term of the lease are sufficient to enable the lessor to recover the cost of the asset plus a return on the investment

Field a geographical area under which, for example, minerals or hydrocarbons are located

Floating charge (England and Wales) a security interest created over the assets and undertaking of a company, including future property, whereby the company retains the right to deal with the charged assets in the ordinary course of its business

Force majeure risks arising from circumstances, generally outside the control of the parties, which entitle one or other party to refrain from performing its contractual obligations

Forward purchase a financing structure whereby one party purchases agreed quantities of future production and/or cash proceeds from the project company, sufficient to produce a return to the purchaser of the purchase price plus an amount equivalent to interest

Full recourse a (conventional) financing structure where the borrower — and possibly guarantors — undertake to be responsible for repaying the loan in full with interest, regardless of the success or failure of the project

Golden share a shareholding interest entitling the holder to exercise a degree of control over certain activities of the company or over the transferability of its shares, usually retained, for example, by a state entity in a newly-privatised enterprise

Governing law the system of law to which the terms and conditions of a contract are subject, either expressly or by operation of the rules of conflict of laws

Gross-up clause — a clause providing for a debtor to make additional payments to the creditor to compensate for withholding taxes or other levies which reduce the amounts actually received by the creditor

Hell-or-high water provisions — provisions which state an unconditional obligation regardless of any event affecting the transaction

IBRD — the International Bank for Reconstruction and Development (the World Bank)

IFC — the International Finance Corporation, the private sector lending agency of the World Bank

Indemnity — an undertaking to protect a person against the consequences of particular circumstances, in particular, for any financial loss

Joint and several liability — liability, for example, under a guarantee given by two or more guarantors, which gives rise to one joint obligation and to as many several obligations as there are obligors, so that each is liable for the payment of the full amount, but performance by one discharges the other

Jurisdiction clause — a clause whereby one or more parties expressly submit to the jurisdiction of specified courts and, commonly, waive any sovereign or other immunities it or they may have

Lender liability — liabilities which may be imposed on lenders as a result of action (or failure to act) on their part, for example, failing to honour a commitment to make a loan

Licence — an authority issued by a state or state entity, for example, to explore for or produce hydrocarbons or minerals in a particular area

Limited recourse — a financing structure in which the lender is relying to some degree on the project assets and cash flows for repayment and debt service without full guarantees from the project company or its sponsors

Margin — the extra percentage rate of interest charged above the relevant basis rate, for example, Libor or Prime rate, in a floating interest rate loan

Material adverse change — an event of default designed to permit acceleration in the event of changes in circumstances which might affect the successful completion of the project, performance of covenants or repayment of the loan

Negative pledge — a covenant whereby a borrower and/or guarantor will undertake not to create or allow the creation of encumbrances on its assets

Non-recourse — meaning the same as "limited recourse", sometimes used to indicate that the lender is placing a particularly high degree of reliance on the project

NPV (net present value) — an estimate of cash flows or the value of production to be generated by a project, net of operating costs and expenses, discounted back to the time of determination

Off-balance-sheet liability — a corporate obligation that does not appear as a liability on the company's balance sheet, for example, lease obligations and take-or-pay contracts

Off-take agreement — a long-term agreement to purchase minimum amounts of the product of a project, at an agreed price; often entered into by one of the project sponsors on a take-or-pay basis

Operating lease — a lease which is not a finance lease — perhaps a short-term lease whereby the lessee uses the asset for only a fraction of its useful life

Pari-passu clause — a covenant whereby the borrower and/or guarantor agrees to ensure that its indebtedness under the loan facility shall rank at least equally with all its other unsecured debt, subject to debts preferred by operation of law, for example, certain taxes and wages

Participation agreement — an agreement whereby one bank agrees to fund all or part of another bank's loan on terms that the other bank will have to repay the funding only if, and to the extent that, it receives repayment from the borrower

Performance bond — a bond or guarantee given by a bank in favour of a project company on behalf of a contractor or supplier of a specified percentage of the value of the relevant contract, for example, construction contract or supply agreement

Pro-rata sharing clause — a clause in a loan or intercreditor agreement whereby banks agree to share amongst themselves amounts received or recovered from the borrower and/or guarantors pro rata to their participation in the financing

Production payment — a financing structure whereby one party purchases an undivided share in the minerals, hydrocarbons or production of the project company in return for periodic production payments by the project company in the production phase of the project

Promissory note — an unconditional promise in writing, signed by the debtor, undertaking to pay a specific sum on demand or at a future date

Put-or-pay agreement — an agreement whereby a supplier undertakes to supply an agreed quantity of materials to the project company and to make payments sufficient to enable the company to obtain alternative supplies in the event of the supplier's failure; often entered into by a project sponsor

Representations — a series of statements of fact and/or law made by one party to an agreement on the basis of which the other party undertakes to enter into the agreement; some or all of the representations may be repeated — or deemed repeated — periodically during the life of the agreement; material inaccuracies will normally constitute an event of default

Royalty — a share of the production or revenues reserved by the grantor of a licence, for example, to exploit hydrocarbons or minerals

Set-off clause	a clause permitting one party (eg, a bank or the agent) to set-off any cash deposits made with it by another (eg, the borrower or guarantor) against amounts owing to it under the loan agreement
Sovereign immunity	the doctrine under which it may be impossible to sue or seize the assets of a state or state entity
SPV (special purpose vehicle)	a company established for a particular purpose, for example, to achieve off-balance sheet or advantageous tax treatment or to isolate the parent's other assets from the creditors of the vehicle
Standby letter of credit	a letter of credit issued by a bank as a form of guarantee, entitling the beneficiary to make a drawing upon presentation of a certificate of non-payment under the guaranteed facility
Subordinated loan	a loan made on terms whereby the lender agrees that some or all payment obligations will rank behind certain other unsecured indebtedness of the borrower
Supplier credit	a financing arrangement under which the supplier agrees to accept deferred payment terms from the buyer and funds itself by discounting or selling the buyer's bills or promissory notes with a bank in its own country
Supply-or-pay agreement	see "put-or-pay agreement" above
Swap	the exchanging of one debt, currency or interest rate for another
Syndicated loan	a loan made available by a group of banks in pre-defined proportions under the same credit facility
Take-and-pay contract	an agreement between a purchaser and a seller whereby the purchaser's obligation to make payments, normally, arises only if the product or service is actually tendered (sometimes used to mean the same as take-or-pay)

Take-or-pay contract	an agreement between a purchaser and a seller whereby the purchaser agrees to pay specified amounts periodically in return for products or services even if there is no delivery of the products or performance of the services
Throughput agreement	an agreement whereby the user of a facility — such as a pipeline — undertakes to the pipeline owner to pass minimum amounts of, say, oil or gas through the pipeline and to pay throughput fees sufficient to cover the owner's costs and debt service obligations
Tolling agreement	an agreement whereby the user of a facility — such as a smelter or refinery — undertakes to the facility owner to supply minimum amounts of raw materials for processing at the facility and to pay tolling fees sufficient to cover the owner's costs and debt service obligations; the user might be obliged to pay a capacity reservation fee even where nothing is put through the facility
Turnkey contract	a contract for the construction of a project and installation of all facilities, providing for the project to be handed over at the point where it is ready for immediate operation
Unitisation agreement	an agreement entered into where a field to be developed is covered by more than one licence with, as a result, different parties being involved; the licensees' interests are unitised to reflect their interest in all the licences covering the field
Withholding tax	tax deductible at source from interest, fees, commissions or dividends
Working capital maintenance agreement	an undertaking, usually given by a parent company, to creditors of its subsidiary to ensure that the subsidiary has sufficient working capital to meet its commitments in accordance with the project and finance documents

Index

D

E

O

PQ

R

Other titles available from IFR Publishing

The Financial Jungle - A Guide to Financial Instruments - 2nd Edition

Extensively revised and updated, this highly regarded publication is a complete guide to all variations of debt, asset-backed, equity and hedging instruments currently in use. Compiled by the international offices of Coopers & Lybrand, this text has been expanded to give a thorough explanation of the nature and practical application of each instrument. The use of diagrams and tables promotes a clearer understanding of complex and sophisticated concepts. It is essential reading for professionals requiring an in-depth understanding of financial instruments.

Authors: Cooper's & Lybrand   Price: £95/US$150

Global Swap Markets

Global Swap Markets complements Swap Financing by providing a timely country-by-country analysis of the markets. This book contains detailed chapters on new and recent developments in swap financing products and applications, market perspectives and regulatory, legal and accounting developments. Topical issues covered include: current developments in major swap currencies, BIS capital adequacy requirements and their impact, the effect of declining bank credit standing on the market, legal, taxation and accounting treatments and implications of the Hammersmith and Fulham litigation in the UK.

Editor: Satyajit Das   Price: £125/US$190

Commodity-linked Derivatives

This title focuses on futures, options, swaps and other sophisticated instruments and promotes a clearer understanding of their structure. It explains the development and theory underlying the instruments with particular attention to recent changes in the markets and future expectations. The book examines exchange-traded contracts, their users and purpose, and the OTC market. For traders and newcomers to the commodities markets, this book provides an up-to-date overview.

Author: Julian Roche   Price: £85/US$130

International Money and Bond Markets

International Money and Bond Markets examines the opportunities for international investment through increasing deregulation in Europe and elsewhere. It studies the background to international investments and examines the role played by the Euromarkets. All aspects of the Euromarkets are covered: Eurobonds, Euro commercial paper, Euronotes (NIFs, RUFs, MTNs etc), as well as innovations in the area of zero-coupon bonds, junk bonds and mortgage-backed securities. Terminology and yield calculations are fully explained. The book also examines the money and bond markets on a country basis concentrating principally on Europe, but also with sections on Australia, Canada, Japan and the US.

Authors: Peter Engström & Johan Lybeck   Price: £85/US$130

IFR Financial Glossary - 3rd Edition

This invaluable publication incorporates many new terms and acronyms which have come into use since the second edition was launched in 1989. The Glossary provides a quick reference source for anyone involved in the financial markets. Alphabetically sorted, the Glossary contains clear and concise contextual definitions of terms used in all the major financial markets.

Price: £33/US$50

Economics: A Guide for the Financial Markets

This book provides a guide to how the financial markets are influenced by and respond to macro-economic policies. It explains the impact of economics on the international bond, equity, money and fx markets. Its clear approach will be invaluable to investors, dealers, salespeople and anyone interested in the relationship between economics and the financial markets. It covers monetary policy, fiscal policy, economic indicators, exchange rates, and features a Who's Who guide to G7 policymakers.

Authors: Neil Mackinnon & Paula Neal, Citibank   Price: £49.50/US$75

Warrants, Options and Convertibles

All aspects of warrants, options and convertibles are covered in this publication. Extensive use of figures and tables lead the reader through this complex subject. Topics treated include: income valuation, present value, parity values, arbitrage, delta hedging, premium expansion and spread trading. Those who find derivatives to be too mathematical and theoretical will be grateful for the use of non-technical analogies to explain the subject. The methodical approach and creative use of examples make this book a suitable training manual.

Author: Quintin Price, James Capel & Co   Price: £75/US$115

Global Credit Analysis

Written by Moody's, the international rating agency, this is the first complete guide to credit risk analysis from a cross-border perspective. It covers major categories of debt issuers in the Euro and domestic debt markets and provides an account of Moody's rating process and symbols, risk forecasting, and analysis of risks in specific securities and in key sectors globally. In addition, it covers Moody's credit ratios, bond and commercial paper default studies and how to access ratings and research.

Author: Moody's Investors Service   Price: £95/US$150

For further information or to order any of these titles, please contact :
Samantha Hannay, IFR Publishing, 11 New Fetter Lane, London EC4A 1JN
Tel: 071 815 3877 Fax: 071 815 3852/3